SPREAD THE WEALTH

More Haves
Fewer Have-Nots

David R. Breuhan

Hamilton Books
A member of
The Rowman & Littlefield Publishing Group
Lanham · Boulder · New York · Toronto · Plymouth, UK

Library of Congress Control Number: 2009935498
ISBN: 978-0-7618-4882-0 (paperback : alk. paper)
eISBN: 978-0-7618-4883-7

To
My Family

For
The Republic

CONTENTS

FIGURES

TABLES

PREFACE

As a private citizen, I had never been involved in public policy. It really never interested me. This work evolved from realizing that neither political party possesses the insight that will cure the nation's systemic problems. Neither party understands the second order effects of their actions. At times, both possess a linear thought process in a non-linear universe. In most instances, political expediency trumps the national interest. The effort herein represents a belief that most issues are self imposed and that our problems do not ultimately require compromise to correct them, but awareness to identify them.

I developed these opinions over thirty years not only through study, but through practical experiences. I spent several years in Europe during the 1980's and served as a Cavalry Commander in Operation Desert Storm. I received a great education from the cadre of the United States Military Academy at West Point and attended graduate school, learning from the instructors in the Department of Finance and Economics at Walsh College. I have managed money for fifteen years at a small firm in Bloomfield Hills, Michigan, where I have been allowed to develop my own style of money management and a good appreciation for the capital markets.

Most important, I have educated roughly 1,000 students, mostly at the graduate level, in finance and economics. Largely without standard textbooks, as many are flawed, I have been able to demonstrate what has, and most importantly, what has not worked in economics and why. In my presentations, I combine knowledge of military and economic history, as well as a strong dose of common sense.

This is a "we can do this" sort of book. The intent is to formulate a public policy dialog between the normally detached American populace, who, after spending a few hours every four years making critical decisions at the polls, place politics aside for the next four. We no longer have that luxury. The decisions we make, or do not make, in the next decade will determine how we live in the next century. Sound decisions will assist us in recovering from the current financial crisis.

This work is designed with the average American in mind, keeping in mind that the average American is far above average. Accuracy and truthfulness are the main objectives. The overall mission is to not only identify issues, but offer solutions for your consideration.

The economic school of thought that will serve as a thread of continuity throughout this book is Austrian economics. The Austrian discipline places importance of capital and its creation. Austrians also believe in classical liberalism, the importance of limited government, private property rights, free trade and a strong and stable currency. We believe that savings is good for both the individual and the nation. Our discipline believes that economics is based on human behavior not econometric modeling.

The "boiling point" which spurred me to write this book occurred following the Bush Administration's imposition of steel tariffs in March 2002. A tariff is a terrible idea at any time. I played a role in getting these removed and reached the right people with unique information.

The second event which triggered me to action was the invasion of Iraq, not so much the invasion itself, but the fact that the National Command Authority was both unwilling and unable to listen to the senior leadership of the Army in the planning and execution of the war. This was more than just a turf war between the heavy forces and the light forces over Army doctrine in the new millennium; it was a failure, once again, to listen to smart people who were attempting to give the proper advice to their superiors. There was an unfortunate pattern in the formulation of domestic and foreign policy. Although the Bush Administration has been replaced by the Obama Administration, similar issues still exist.

I am going to attempt to highlight our government's policy shortcomings and bring historical examples of what works and what does not. I have a deep and growing concern that the current path on which we have embarked ignores the very basic laws of practical economics and will bring about needless consequences in the future if market reforms are not embraced. This need for reform transcends political parties and economic schools of thought. The ideas that will be presented are not radical; they are actually more historical.

The reforms of government and good policies must result from the people making legitimate, non-monetary demands from their elected officials. Politicians who do not reform the government should not be reelected. The "push" from the citizens must be very strong. Reforms will not take place as a result of campaign speeches and promises. Politicians repay favors by making changes in the law to reward donors. A political and economic renaissance must come from the citizens of the Republic. This is where hope rests.

With respect to the standard of living, we must increase it rather quickly, and that needs to happen globally. The increase, *not the redistribution of wealth*, will alleviate much of the world's anger and misunderstanding. This can only happen by opening the trading lanes to allow prosperity to flourish. It is only through the reinforcement of private property rights and increasing specialization that the tempest of anger, born from poverty, will be eliminated.

Although the book remains broad, the theme of free trade, stable currency, private property rights and sound policy resonates throughout.

I wrote this book from February 2005 through July 2009. It was only through the vision of Hamilton Books and its parent Rowman & Littlefield who understood the need and timeliness of this work that it has been published. Thank you to Jonathon Sisk, Publisher of Rowman & Littlefield. Thank you to Judith Rothman, Brooke Bascietto, Brian DeRocco, Julia Loy and Paula Smith-Vanderslice at Hamilton Books. To Diane Nine, my literary agent, who provided wise counsel and displayed great patience enduring rejections from forty publishers; accept my profound thanks for your guidance and coaching throughout this process.

Thanks to my wonderful wife Elisabeth, who supported this effort and the years of research and work to bring it to publication.

I would like to acknowledge assistance provided by several great friends and fine professionals who, over the course of many years, rendered sage advice and editing to make this work possible.

My friend and West Point classmate Brigadier General William Rapp did a meticulous job editing the first draft of this work. He understood the intent and ensured that the presentation of the work flowed in a logical and orderly fashion.

Beth Geno, "my volunteer," spent months on this project. Her prowess and common sense helped me to bring a better read to the general public. She edited the work and formatted it for final publication. Thanks to Tom Goral who offered sage technical guidance.

Thanks to Major John Gossart, who found time to proof the rough draft and final version, despite his deployment to Iraq. He made some great recommendations.

Bruce Byrd, Brian Pradko, Joseph Tocco, Scott Sipple, Daniel Quick, and Harry Veryser provided me with sound guidance. They all read the work and assisted in the editing process. Thanks to James Scapa who edited the work and encouraged me to "present evidence." David Littmann provided me with very wise counsel. I am grateful to Major Steven Carroll, Gregory Suhajda, Adam Pradko and Austin Everett who found time to proof the final draft.

My sincere thanks to you, the reader, who will set aside time from your other many endeavors to spend time with mine.

My hope is that you will act on the information presented.

David R. Breuhan
State of Michigan
July 4, 2009

ACKNOWLEDGEMENTS

I have to give praise to the Department of Social Sciences at the United States Military Academy at West Point. The "Sosh" Department was my respite as a non-engineer at an engineering school. When Thomas Jefferson developed West Point in 1802 he needed a professional cadre of officers to fight the nation's wars, but also engineers to develop the frontier. As we used to joke, West Point was 180 years of tradition, unhampered by progress. Thirty of forty classes we studied were required courses. With no aptitude and even less interest, I struggled through courses like thermo-fluid dynamics, solid mechanics and electrical engineering. The Sosh and History Departments were my refuge. These departments and the Academy made me very aware of the world, its history and most importantly, how to be a problem solver.

I had some great courses with excellent instructors. Thanks go to Major Ed Kleckley, who as an instructor in my junior year allowed me to write an essay that was later published in *Defense Science*. The paper finished first in a category on ground defense. This was a big deal at the time to be published as a cadet. The Sosh Department was quite happy. The publisher, Robert daCosta, later visited West Point and told me that my paper was in the final running against that of an Army general. He decided that the essays looked about the same and he thought that the cadet should have it. Many thanks for my first "break."

Colonel (ret.) Andrew Krepenevich trained me in the field of national security studies. Colonel (ret.) Ken Allard allowed me to join the National Model United Nations group. In the spring of 1984, we competed against other universities in New York. We won that year. I was with the group called the International Security Assistance Staff which provided the students of the conference updates on global political and military affairs. Thanks to Colonel (ret.) Joe Collins who taught a great Soviet Security studies course. It was an excellent "capstone" course tying the strategic reasons for serving the nation to the tactical realities of being a lieutenant along the iron curtain. Thanks to my academic advisor Colonel (ret.) Asa A. "Ace" Clark IV, who provided me with wise advice in my cadet career.

My friend and squad leader, Brigadier General John W. "Mick" Nicholson, Jr. instilled in me a profound sense of duty and a deep appreciation that Academy graduates had a special obligation to the nation. Mick would later serve as the Deputy Commander of NATO forces in Southern Afghanistan.

To Lieutenant General (ret.) Willard W. Scott, Jr. our Superintendent, who left us with two profound thoughts: "Excellence is the exercise" and "As sons and daughters of God, we are never truly the ones in charge." His passing this year was met with much sadness by many graduates of West Point. The nation is better from his service.

A special thanks to William R. Raiford, U.S. Military Academy Class of 1952. Bill is the past president of the Society of the Cincinnati and a Trustee Emeritus at West Point. He befriended me at the Thayer Award Dinner for Jimmy Doolittle at West Point in 1983. Bill provided me with wise counsel in my 20's and knowing him made me a better person. A special friend and great American, he has provided many services to the United States as a soldier in the Korean War, diplomat and a trusted advisor to those in Washington. He set a fine example.

General (ret.) Montgomery C. Meigs, my first squadron commander, with the First Squadron, First Cavalry, told me that an officer "must possess intellectual curiosity" and selected me for two critical positions that would greatly impact my life. The first was to serve as platoon leader in C Troop and work for Captain Terry Wolff. Terry was a great commander. A steady, confident officer, he found time to educate a young lieutenant. He sat me down in his office right away and told me that he was going to structure me for success. Talk about putting someone at ease upon arrival. Terry was a master at multi-tasking; long before it became a household word.

Terry would later serve as Special Assistant to the President and Director for Iraq and Afghanistan on the National Security Council. He currently serves as the Commanding General of the First Armored Division, the unit we served in together. General Meigs would eventually serve as commander of U.S. Seventh Army (Europe) and head the IED task force for President George W. Bush.

My second assignment was to "do Boeselager." This competition was NATO's Olympics of Scouting, which involved 24 teams from 14 nations, hosted annually by the West German Army. Shunned by other lieutenants, this job was looked at as a career killer and written off as a silly sports event. I thought it would be great to give it a try. I couldn't have had a better assignment. I got to work with our German allies hand in hand for three years. Our partnership unit, Panzeraufklarungsbatalion 4, from Roding, Bayern (Bavaria) assisted us for many years in preparation for victory in 1988. The company commanders Alfons Ebneth and Peter Kallert were the best of friends, great tacticians and wonderful counselors. Hans Graf, their first sergeant, was certainly a real soldier. My good friend Hubertus Hilgendorff of Eutin provided our team wise counsel and good tactical insight on ground reconnaissance. Sadly, years later he would die in a car accident. I was fortunate to have spoken to him only a month before. He gave me a book after our victory on German reconnaissance forces entitled, *Spahtrupp Bleibt am Feind*. He was a wonderful ally of the United States.

I am grateful to the men of Recon Platoon, HHT, First Squadron, First Cavalry who represented the United States from 1986 to 1988 in the Boeselager Competition. These soldiers were outstanding in all areas and it was a privilege to lead them. They taught me a lot.

Colonel (ret.) Emmett "Bob" White was our squadron commander from 1986-1988. His "hands off" leadership style made our victory over our arch rivals, the 11th Armored Cavalry Regiment, especially sweet. He certainly had a lot of patience; more than I would have had with me.

Mention is deserved to Brigadier General (ret.) Thomas White, who led the 11th Cavalry during my tenure in Germany. I attended many joint meetings with him. His bombastic and confident leadership style was exactly what the army needed defending the Fulda Gap in the Cold War. His boys really looked up to him. Brigadier General White would later serve as the Secretary of the Army.

Thanks to General (ret.) Wayne Downing, former commander of the Special Operations Command. I met General Downing in the fall of 1988 when he was the Deputy Commander of the Army's Training and Doctrine Command. He allowed me to develop a plan for a scout training school based on lessons from Boeselager and arranged for me to be interviewed for a video entitled, "Train to Win," which was distributed Army wide. He wrote me a personal note which ended it with, "Keep thinking important thoughts." General Downing passed away a few years ago. I still remember his note to this day.

My command in Operation Desert Storm was with the men of B Troop, 1st Squadron, 3rd Armored Cavalry Regiment. We all made it back safely, the goal of any commander in war time. We made the best of a situation that we really had not expected. The whole outfit deserves credit. What a great group to go to war with. America's finest.

I am most grateful to the former members of the Department of Finance and Economics at Walsh College for the first rate graduate education and most importantly training me to recognize which policies in the United States need to be most improved. My wife and my sister-in-law, Paige Pradko, played a vital role in making me attend graduate school. I was dead set against it, for no good reason. Women often know best.

Profound thanks to Harry Veryser, the Department Chairman of graduate economics at the University of Detroit Mercy. Harry led our department at Walsh College for twenty years. Professor Veryser has impacted the lives of tens of thousands of students and many instructors. He has amassed a wealth of knowledge in all fields of economics and although he has taught us the Austrian discipline, he reached his viewpoints only after having studied the Keynesian school and that of the Monetarists. Harry represents the finest in the profession. He allowed us a wide berth in our teaching styles and content. It was his influence that allowed me to rapidly change professions and find my new path. His training allowed me to directly assist in removing the steel tariffs using the combined knowledge of history and how markets operate.

My key instructors: Paul Ballew, Joseph Weglarz, Don Byrne and Charles S. "Terry" Davis III had a profound impact on me and trained me well. They taught me cause and effect, inductive logic and the understanding of "practical economics" as opposed to "theory economics." i.e. Keynesian. To the Walsh College reference librarians Nancy Brzozowski and Barb Koch, many thanks for finding information that made my graduate courses very interesting for my students.

To Thomas Donlan and the staff at *Barron's*, Richard Burr of *The Detroit News* and Mary Kramer at *Crain's Detroit Business*, accept my warm and profound thank you for embracing my ideas and allowing me to reach your bright readers. Sincere thanks to the editors of the *Marine Corps Gazette* and *Infantry Magazine* for publishing my work on small unit tactics.

To the editors of *The Wall Street Journal* and *The New York Times*, my sincere thanks for 29 years of practical education. I began reading both papers while a cadet at the U.S. Military Academy in 1980 and they remain present in my life every day. While presenting a different view of the world, they agree on two vitally important policies: free trade and a strong dollar.

A final thank you to my classmate Lieutenant Colonel (ret.) Richard Hewitt, who as Chair of the Economics Staff with the Department of Social Sciences at West Point, allowed me to return to "my department" on several occasions to brief his dedicated officers on current economic issues and lecture the cadets on personal financial planning. Returning to the Military Academy was a most rewarding experience.

To all, I am most grateful.

CHAPTER 1
YOU'LL GET YOUR MEETING

Government will only make the right decision
when it has exhausted all other possibilities.

By way of introduction, this chapter illustrates how any of us, working diligently as private citizens, can make a difference in policy. The current economic situation in the United States requires your direct and immediate involvement to educate government officials who are wrongly attempting to resolve issues through centralized planning. Historically, these types of actions only lead to further distortions and expanded control. The United States is a functioning republic and relies heavily on the actions of common citizens to help it achieve its full potential. This chapter may help provide you with ideas to use as a reference as you progress through the remainder of the book. You can make a profound difference in the course of our country. Your wisdom is urgently needed by the government.

My foray into the steel tariff fight began with a question and ended 16 months and 500 hours of pro-bono work later with a return phone call from a member of the President's Council of Economic Advisers, followed by an e-mailed briefing.

By June 2002, the Federal Reserve had cut interest rates eleven times in an attempt to get the economy going. This type of monetary policy lowers the cost to borrowers, thereby making capital more plentiful and increasing disposable personal income for individuals and net income for corporations. The net effect on the stock market is positive. Lower costs lead to higher profits and the anticipation of improved earnings will cause the market to rise today in expectation of what will happen in the future.

Despite these interest rate cuts, the market moved downward. As a an economist with an understanding of history, I began to look for macro trends that would have impacted the capital markets so strongly as to negate the Federal Reserve's interest rate cuts.

Steel tariffs went into effect on March 20, 2002. The next question, when did the market peak? I looked for peaks and found that the Dow Jones Industrial Average had peaked on March 19th, the day before the steel tariffs took effect. It was apparent to me that this was no coincidence. It took a few days to get organized.

I drew a flow chart on a yellow sheet of lined paper. Started with President Bush at the top and the people I knew at the bottom. There was a lot of space in between. An almost impossible task and I knew it. I took this action because I had information that few others had, both in government and academics. This information concerned how markets discount the future value of stocks and adjust the present value accordingly. Specifically, how the Smoot Hawley Tariff of 1930 caused the market to crash in October 1929, before the bill actually became law. I needed to get this information to the President, since most theories on the Great Depression involved the adverse effects of the gold standard or the Federal Reserve's restrictive monetary policies before the crash.

My strategy would involve two courses of action. I would publish, lecture and give interviews in public and find in roads into the policy making venues privately in Washington. I also realized that from the outset and all the way through this campaign, or as others called it, a crusade, I would be unable to get in front of decision makers. If I couldn't get into their offices, I would have to get into their homes, preferably on the weekend, when they would have time to read. I began to think of national weekend publications.

Other groups had been involved in this effort prior to my joining the fray. Organizations such as the Precision Metal Forming Association (PMA) and Motor Equipment Manufacturing Association (MEMA) were lobbying congress. Many members of congress strongly represented manufacturers in their districts. I focused on the fact that the post September 11th peak of the Dow Jones Industrial Average occurred the day before the steel tariffs took effect. I would use the Smoot Hawley Tariff's impact on the market seven decades earlier and warn the Administration that promised European and Asian retaliation against the steel tariff would cause the market to crash. I developed this strategy over the course of a few months and the key was finding someone to listen.

In June 2002, my very first call went to Anne Mervenne, Chief of Staff and advisor to Michigan's first lady, Michelle Engler. I had met Anne several years earlier at a conservative function called The First

Saturday Society. This group boasted no dues, no by laws, no officers. It was a loosely-run and tight knit group, organized by some loyal Republicans, Harry Veryser and Joe Katz, just to name a few.

My instinct was to get guidance on who to talk to in the White House and how best to get a response and not get "blown off." I thought this would be more easily accomplished with a referral. To my surprise, there would be none coming. Anne informed me that Michigan was not in good standing in the White House. John McCain had bested George Bush in the 2000 Michigan primary and the state went for Al Gore in the general election. In the Senate, we were represented by Debbie Stabenow and Carl Levin, both liberal Democrats. Further, Republican John Engler was a lame duck currently on the "outs" with the administration because of a spat over health care issues and a lack of federal funding. In short, the state had little clout in the Administration.

Anne advised me to use the business community to contact senior administration officials. I would do this, but also use a direct method.

My first thought was to notify the press. I thought CNBC would be the most receptive, since this is what they are supposed to do for a living. Following several months making little progress with faxes, voicemails, e-mails and no call back, I gave up on them. I can remember talking with one producer and asking her what determined the price of a stock. She said, "Are you trying to lecture me?" To which I responded, "No, I am asking you a question."

I remember renowned investor Peter Lynch once quipping that, "CNBC was MTV in suits" and that allowed me to keep my sense of humor. I later went through my tariff drawer and was amazed at how many producers I contacted with vital information proving the market's reaction and direct relationship to the tariff. They never listened. Not being a member of "the club" or paying $30,000 to a marketing firm to put me in front of a producer did not help.

I called the White House and asked to speak to Josh Bolten's executive assistant, Carol Thompson. Mr. Bolten was the Deputy Chief of Staff to the President. I thought it would be better to start with him, rather than Andrew Card, who was the President's Chief of Staff. Carol wanted to refer me to the National Security Council but I asked her not to since my information was too important and would sit on a staffer's desk for weeks. She agreed and accepted my fax and several calls afterward. She was a great listener.

I learned a lot the first summer. My father told me, "you can't buy experience, but you have to pay for it." I certainly paid for it in July

2002. I made the mistake of forgetting brevity and sent lengthy faxes to different offices. I left wordy messages, especially to Larry Lindsey, Assistant to the President for Economic Policy. Basically, I bothered him every week. One day in the fall, our receptionist called to my office saying, "hey, there is someone from the White House on the phone." It was Jeannie Russell, Larry Lindsey's assistant. Just to get a return call from someone was an accomplishment.

I began writing an editorial focusing on the correlation of the steel tariff to the market and its effects on future earnings. I tried *The Wall Street Journal* and other publications, to no avail. I tried *The Detroit News*. The editor, Richard Burr, said "you may be on to something." While I was writing this, I cold called the local radio stations to determine their level of interest. As it turned out, they were very interested.

In July 2002, my first local breakthrough came via Detroit radio on the Mitch Albom show on WJR 760 and the CBS affiliate WWJ 950. Two months later, the essay ran in *The Detroit News*. Richard Burr had a graph showing the market's behavior for the past year. A picture was worth 1,000 words.

It was just by luck that I received an invitation to go to a private home to raise money for Congressman Joe Knollenberg. I didn't know at the time that he was opposed to the tariffs, but I made a few calls and dropped a briefing off to his staff at the event. I later spent thirty minutes with him in his district office. We discussed both macro and micro effects of the tariff. I provided him with historical data on the effects of the Smoot Hawley Tariff of 1930 and the direct correlation to the market crash of 1929.

Beginning in September 2002, I gave many free educational lectures. I briefed the Precision Metal Forming Association (PMA) of Southeast Michigan and a manufacturing group at the Meadowbrook Country Club. Congressman Don Manzullo of Illinois keynoted the Meadowbrook event. I spoke to a member of the National Security Council the day following my PMA brief. I told him that I had just met with forty CEOs of Michigan manufacturing companies and their businesses were being decimated by high steel prices due to the tariff. He told me that his data did not correlate to my information. We spoke for an hour and I could not convince him of the growing problem in manufacturing.

I had breakfast with David Littmann, Senior Economist from Comerica Bank and Joe Katz. I met with Paul Welday, the Oakland County Republican chairman. Randall Thompson stopped by the office for a two hour meeting. He was with a conservative organization. I met with a reporter from *The Detroit News* in the city of Royal Oak, for a morning coffee, with no result. I briefed the First Saturday Society. I spoke to Brain Wesbury, a well respected economist in Chicago and Dan Gibson at the National Association of Manufacturers. I made many calls to the Bush Administration including Merrill Hughes in Mary Matlin's office and Rob LaKritz at Treasury. I spoke numerous times to Mary Long-necker in George Will's office and tried to reach Larry Kudlow.

With no national publishing luck, I called the economics editor of *Barron's*, Gene Epstein. He referred me to Tom Donlan, the editorial page editor. Tom stated in an e-mail that he had just run a piece on the subject of steel tariffs, but wished me luck elsewhere. Elsewhere would eventually be *Barron's*, but it would take nearly another year of honing my trade and other failures before going back in May 2003. The old adage was true, it wasn't intellect, it was persistence.

After having some success publishing locally, giving lectures and meeting a few folks my efforts began to slow down. The markets were tanking and my business was terrible. No one was paying for my consulting services and investment flows were down. The market would eventually bottom on October 9, 2002.

I attended a fundraiser in the fall in Dearborn, Michigan. President Bush gave the keynote speech. I sat in on a briefing by Karl Rove given to about fifty manufacturers. At the event, I met John Guzik of the prestigious law firm, Williams Mullen. He and I would become close allies through the rest of the process. He told me not to ask Rove any tariff questions and that this event was a fund raiser, not an ambush. We would get a meeting about tariffs and now was not the time. I had known him only five minutes, but I trusted his instinct. During this campaign I referred to John as "Mr. Inside" and I was "Mr. Outside."

Following the President's speech, I lined up to meet him. I could have completed my flowchart that I made earlier that summer, but I kept my powder dry and introduced myself as an Army Captain who had served for his father in the First Gulf War. He looked me in the eyes as I spoke to him. I told him, this time, give them everything we had. He said, "Don't worry, we will."

My New Year's resolution for 2003 was to stop my own steel tariff campaign. That lasted only a few days as I received several calls in January asking for my research or assistance. Like it or not, I was committed.

In January 2003, *Barron's* published my letter to the editor about the tariffs. It was a start. On March 26th, the World Trade Organization ruled against the United States on the steel tariffs. The Administration vowed to appeal.

In April, I went online to the United States International Trade Commission's web site and found that there was going to be a hearing on the effects of the tariffs on the steel consuming industry. I thought I should attend and present my findings on the markets. I sent fourteen copies of my briefing and shortly thereafter, received an invitation to testify.

I traveled to Washington to brief the Commission on June 19, 2003. I went as a private citizen, representing only myself. My thought was quite simple. Ally yourself with no one and be above the fray. I would be briefing on the first panel with CEO's and staffers from Metaldyne, Federal Mogul, Delphi and other manufacturers. The commission's staff really did not have a place for an economics guy with a room full of metal benders. So, I suggested I could end the first panel briefing.

When I initially contacted the administration staff, I had been told I would be given ten minutes to testify. I structured my briefing to meet that guidance. When I arrived that morning, I was told I'd have five minutes. My initial thought went to calculating how much money I'd spent out of pocket, just to have my presentation cut in half. I decided to ditch my overhead slide presentation and just brief from the slides I had copied.

I walked around the tables where our panel were seated and handed out my briefing. I gave one to John Guzik and he asked, "Where's your testimony?" I said, "Well, this is it, I'm giving a briefing." He responded, "That's great!"

I didn't realize that the people who were testifying would be reading a five minute statement. My bullet briefing would be unique with charts and graphs. Maybe the commission would have to face the fact that they helped tank the equity markets in 2002 and so far in 2003, the markets had not recovered past the March 19, 2002, post September 11th peak.

There were probably seventy people seated in chairs behind the first panel. I did not bring copies for them, but managed to go back to the panel's tables and take two briefings back and hand them to reporters from Reuters and Bloomberg. I told them I always enjoyed their coverage and that there was original research in this briefing that tied the market's performance to the passage of the steel tariffs.

The panel began testifying in order around 9:30 am. As members of Congress arrived, they would be promptly inserted into the order. The best briefing came from Congressman Steven Mark Kirk of Illinois. I think he used the word stupid or idiotic three times in ten minutes. He really gave it to the commission. He stood, too, and was quite animated. It was definitely the highlight of the morning.

My turn finally came. I was actually glad to stand up. We had been sitting since 9:30 am; it was well past 1 pm. During the presentation, most remained seated, I stood for three reasons. First, the constitution begins with the phrase, "We the people." The folks in Washington only govern with our consent and I did not consent to this policy. Second, my tax dollars paid their salary. Third, after spending my own money to testify and losing roughly one third of my income the previous year to this endeavor, I was not going to have the commission be above me. I would be at eye level with them.

Five minutes provided little time for humor, but my opening line was, "I appreciate being able to come here and challenge a policy of the government. It wasn't so long ago in history that you could always enter a room like this, but you may never come out." Everyone laughed.

I continued with an overview of international trade dating from 1776, dividing events into positive and negative. Only spending about 45 seconds on this, I emphasized the Constitution's establishing free trade between the states, an idea borrowed from Adam Smith's *Wealth of Nations*.

I discussed Smoot Hawley's effects on the markets and global trade. This tariff adversely affected the capital markets and decreased global trade in the early 1930's. The Smoot Hawley Tariff and the steel tariff were in the wrong column of history. That did not go over well.

The next page pointed out the difference between items in an economy that had lag effects, such as interest rate hikes and actions which had an immediate effect, such as a weak dollar or tariffs. I briefly discussed the difference between cyclical economic items, such as one-time events and structural impediments to growth, which inhibit growth until they are removed.

A chart followed, which illustrated the increase in steel prices from $210 in December 2001 to $400 per ton in July 2002. This was hot rolled steel, commonly used to make car parts. The Administration touted their action as a 30 percent tariff on imported steel, not 90 percent. The charts also showed the numbers of individuals employed in the steel industry and the manufacturing sector. In one year, manufacturers lost more jobs than in the entire steel industry. The data was from the Bureau of Labor Statistics, an impartial source.

Next, I addressed the reactions of the capital markets, the steel and lumber markets and also covered the drop in the S&P 500 from March 2002 until May 2003. This was over $2 trillion in market capitalization and some of this was due to the steel tariffs.

I included the copy of my September 3, 2002, *Detroit News* editorial. This essay showed the graph of the Dow Jones Industrial Average from September 2001 to August 2002. As I explained this chart, I stated to the chair of the committee that the Dow had reached its post September 11th peak on March 19, 2002, the day before the steel tariffs took effect and that this was no coincidence. Markets anticipate future earnings and tariffs reduce them. My impression was that no one on the panel believed this. The chair of the committee actually smiled.

A graph illustrating the structure of production followed. This diagram showed what the CEO's were explaining to the committee, verbally. Simply put, the steel tariffs had driven the price of hot rolled steel up roughly ninety percent in seven months. Purchasers of the steel absorbed this cost entirely. They were unable to pass this cost on to their customers because the big three Detroit automakers and other major purchasers had mandated that in order to keep their contracts, these suppliers had to cut their costs roughly five percent per year to maintain their relationship. The larger producers had the power to go overseas and buy parts from foreign suppliers and bypass the tariff. Unable to pass costs along and not willing to lose their relationships, many auto parts suppliers borrowed money or lived off of their balance sheets as long as they could. The manufacturing sector began to implode. This was not the fault of cheap imports. It was a self inflicted wound.[1]

Figure 1.1

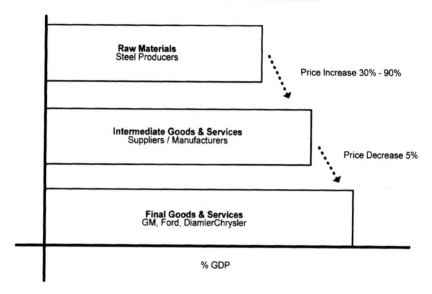

The Structure of Production

Raw Materials
Steel Producers

Price Increase 30% - 90%

Intermediate Goods & Services
Suppliers / Manufacturers

Price Decrease 5%

Final Goods & Services
GM, Ford, DiamlerChrysler

% GDP

The table below illustrated how the tariff created a 90 percent increase in price of steel, not a 30 percent increase.[2]

Table 1.1

Selected Steel Prices
December 2001 - July 2002

Items	2001 Dec	2002 Jan	Feb	Mar	Apr	May	Jun	Jul
Hot-rolled steel sheet (Midwest, $/ton)	210	220	230	260	290	320	340	400
Cold-rolled steel sheet (Midwest, $/ton)	300	310	320	370	380	410	435	525
HD galvanized steel sheet (Midwest, $/ton)	320	330	330	380	415	425	445	535

My five minutes ended and I thanked the committee for their time. I returned to my seat and about an hour of questioning followed. We were then dismissed.

I promptly hopped into a cab and rode to visit Congressman Joe Knollenberg's staff. I visited with Craig Albright, his legislative aide. I gave him the steel tariff brief and choked down a salad before hopping on the metro and riding out to Alexandria to meet with K.C. Jones of the Republican National Committee. K.C. was friendly and was a good listener. I gave her a bound briefing and spent an hour with her. She got the importance and told me she would forward the briefing on to someone who may help. Never asked who that would be, but she struck me as someone who was well connected and that is where I left it.

The visit with K.C. was the final stop of the day. I returned home and promptly deleted all my e-mail addresses from my tariff campaign. I was thoroughly disappointed with the whole affair in Washington and I resolved for the second time to quit my personal campaign. I did not think that the International Trade Commission believed anything anyone said. My feelings were that the hearings were simply a charade, meant to appease rather than investigate. The meetings had been arranged by steel consuming industries, but the steel producers had the following day to rebut everything we had tried to do. My pause in this campaign lasted two weeks.

In late June, I received an e-mail from Tom Donlan, the editorial page editor of *Barron's,* stating that he wanted to run my essay. I had submitted another opinion piece in late May. This was great news. I had always enjoyed reading my *Barron's* on Saturday afternoon. I read Tom's essays first and then the rest of the letters and op-eds. Gene Epstein was always a good read, too. I was really happy that I would get a chance to share a page with the likes of these folks from New York and Washington. This also fit perfectly into my strategy of: if you can't get into their office, get into their homes. You never knew who would read this.

Tom made a few suggestions, telling me to move the front of the essay to the back and the back to the front. I managed to do this in about four hours and sent the final copy back to him. He told me to make myself available during the first week of August so that one of the copy editors would be able to contact me.

Sure enough, I received a call from Anita Peltonen, Tom's copy editor in New York. As we went back and forth, the copy appeared to be an actual living document. In all of my previous military and civilian writings, I had not experienced this. As we got closer to the deadline on Friday afternoon, I asked if we were still ok on space and time. Space was no problem, I would later learn why and time wasn't an issue since this would be sent out via satellite to printers worldwide. Welcome to the twenty first century. We finished around 3:30 pm.

On August 11, 2003, I watched as the mail truck neared the house and walked out to get my *Barron's*. I was delighted that it was on the last page, where Tom Donlan's editorials ran. He was on vacation. I now knew why Anita did not have an issue with space. The piece looked great and the title could not have been more suiting: "Tariffs and the Party of Free Trade." This was the title I had asked for and with a little nudging, I had been allowed to run with it.

On Tuesday, *The Wall Street Journal* ran its own editorial on the tariffs and cited pieces from my op-ed. *The Journal* wanted to own this issue, so I had no luck in getting published there, but as they were owned by the same parent company as *Barron's*, Dow Jones, they had ready access to my data. I viewed this as another salvo at the Administration, so if they wanted my stuff more power to them. Since this information was in the public domain, my attitude was "let's go!"

Two weeks later, I received a call from Mary Kramer, editor of *Crain's Detroit Business*. She read my article in *Barron's* and wished to do an interview with me. The best quotation from the interview was that President Bush was acting more like Herbert Hoover than Ronald Reagan.

On September 20th, the International Trade Commission's released their mid-point review. The findings were not in our favor. The commission found that the steel tariffs impacted the overall economy by a fraction of one percent of GDP.[3] There was no mention of the effect on the equity market or the number of firms that collapsed. The issue was far from over.

I decided to make two final phone calls. The first would be to Dr. N. Gregory Mankiw, Chairman of the President's Council of Economic Advisers. My thought process on calling him was reached in the form of a question. Who would listen? A university professor, since he is accustomed to taking questions from students. Professor Mankiw was on a two-year leave of absence from Harvard. He had published a major economics textbook and wrote a column in *Fortune*. He was well respected in his field and was one of those academics who actually "got it."

My second call would go to Secretary of State Colin Powell. I, well, we all served under General Powell during Operation Desert Storm. I was a cavalry troop commander in Third Cavalry and he was Chairman of the Joint Chiefs of Staff. He was far removed from me in the chain of command, but all soldiers know their commanders have what is known as an "open door policy." This enables troopers of all ranks to make an appointment with their boss and air their grievances. I had also attended a function in the spring of 2000 entitled, "An Evening with Rochester College" where General Powell was the guest speaker. During the course of his speech, he mentioned he had a special place in his heart for the soldiers that served in Desert Storm.

To further add to my chances of getting through, I had one "ace" to open the door. During my service in Europe with 1-1 Cavalry, I had been selected to participate in the Boeselager competition in 1986 as the VII Corps patrol leader and in 1987 and 1988 as the team captain and primary training officer. Not a well known competition to the lay person, this five day annual event hosted by the West German Army comprised 24 teams from 14 NATO nations. This competition was the equivalent to the super bowl for reconnaissance forces in Western Europe.

General Powell had been the V Corps commander whose 11th Armored Cavalry had won in 1987. My team, from VII Corps, won in 1988. Although he had been in Washington in 1987 after giving up his corps command early to become Ronald Reagan's National Security Adviser, he mentioned his happiness of learning of V Corps win in his book, *My American Journey*.[4] Although steel tariffs had little to do with his day to day affairs it involved international relations. I knew that he was a good listener and had commanded the same troops I did. A long shot, but after cold calling the White House, I had little to lose.

On September 15th, I called the White House and asked for the Chairman of the Council of Economic Advisers and then asked for Dr. Mankiw's executive assistant. I introduced myself and explained the situation and then asked, "Would Dr. Mankiw read something from someone he never heard of?" She said, "Yes, he would."

I faxed my *Barron's* piece, my *Detroit News* essay with market graph, a one page bullet briefing entitled, "The Effects of Tariffs," and my biography, just to let him know I wasn't some nut from Detroit. After a year of this, I learned that my early faxes to different agencies were disposed of quickly; brevity was the key.

On September 29th, I received a voice mail message from Dr. Philip Levy, Greg Mankiw's Senior Trade Advisor and a Professor of Economics at Yale. His question to me was direct: what would happen to the U.S. markets if we did not lift the steel tariffs and the Europeans and other nations retaliated against us, all at once? I said it was possible for the Dow Jones Industrial Average to drop 1,000 to 2,000 points very rapidly.

We spoke for about forty minutes and exchanged ideas on the nature of trade. I spoke of the Smoot Hawley Tariff and the market crash of 1929. I emphasized that this was a depression caused by an implosion of global trade and the Revenue Act of 1932, not the gold standard or monetary tightening. We discussed the depression at length and the rise of economic nationalism throughout the 1920's and 1930's, with all of the ignorance and poor decisions that placed the world into a situation where it was easy for Hitler to come to power.

I recalled the great Age of Classical Liberalism, where wages doubled and doubled again, and prices dropped. The great economic progress during the nineteenth century in the United States and Great Britain were due in large part to free trade, stable currency and private property rights. I mentioned that Article I, Section 9 of the U.S. Constitution established free trade between the states, an idea adopted from Adam Smith's *The Wealth of Nations* in 1776.

I offered to send him a three page bullet point briefing entitled, "Potential Economic Consequences of the Continued Trade Policies of the United States," which he accepted.

My concluding thoughts to Dr. Levy were that this issue wasn't about steel tariffs; it was about all of the needless suffering and 50 million deaths in the Second World War. I ended with a question: "If we are going to make the same mistakes as our grandparent's generation, than why are we here?"

There was a long pause, and then Philip said, "I'll tell Greg and he'll tell the President." And after many days and nights, that's all I needed to hear. I knew that with my information, combined with the efforts of manufacturers, Members of Congress and insiders like John Guzik, we would carry the day.

The announcement came on December 4, 2003, as Scott McClellan, the White House Press Secretary, gave a brief statement from the press room that the tariffs would be lifted. PBS reported the news with the header, "President Bush Lifts Steel Tariffs to Avert Trade War."[5] Joe Katz had e-mailed me a *Washington Post* article the Monday prior that this would be the case. Craig Albright from Joe Knollenberg's staff sent me the official notification that afternoon. It was a great day. The Dow Jones Industrial Average finally crossed its March 19, 2002, close of 10,635.25 a few weeks later. Free trade increases earnings and earnings drive markets.

The steel tariff fight provided me with insights into the workings of government and politics. Despite the many roadblocks, I learned some very important lessons. First, the government needs your help. Second, the top people in any administration may never receive the correct information in order to make a good decision. Third, watch your back. There are many people who do not have the nation's best interest at heart, only their own. Fourth, politics is an industry with its own language and customs. Finally, there are many people who work very hard at low pay and really try to do the right thing. This was a most worthwhile endeavor.

Ignoring trade policy is a mistake often made by governments. In order to foster a positive macroeconomic environment, our elected officials must adhere to basic principles that have worked throughout history. Chapter two provides a base of solid economic principles and key elements of successful free market economies. If adopted and adhered to by governments, their populace would be well served.

CHAPTER 2
IGNORE THESE AT YOUR PERIL

We can displace volumes of myths with paragraphs of truth.

Like it or not, the United States must be the nation that leads the world into an age of global stability and prosperity. Americans must be fully supportive of this effort. In a republic, citizens usually vote their pocketbook. Corporations give donations based on their political return on investment. Governments have attempted to replace the actions and functions of markets and have made bad situations worse. In many instances, government actions exacerbate inequalities at home and abroad. Global reform can only be accomplished after we achieve domestic success.

This chapter has two sections: seventeen principles and nine key elements for successful free market economies. First, seventeen principles are listed that form guidelines to be followed implementing sound public policy. Following the seventeen principles is a table illustrating nine key elements that are needed for a successful free market economy. An explanation follows of how the government distorts these elements and what is a result of this distortion. The table is indirectly related to the principles and illustrates macroeconomic cause and effect.

Before viewing the principles, it may be useful to offer a brief overview on the economic philosophy of this book and that of two alternative theories, which are more widely known and taught.

The economic school of thought that will serve as a thread of continuity throughout this book is Austrian economics. The Austrian discipline places importance on capital and its creation. Austrians also believe in classical liberalism, not modern liberalism, and the importance of limited government, private property rights, free trade and a strong and stable currency. Austrians believe that savings is good for both individuals and the nation. Austrians share the views of Thomas Jefferson and Andrew Jackson on the hazards of central banking. This philosophy views a central bank as being responsible for inflation and ultimately destroying the currency. Austrians support a gold standard. This discipline believes that economics is based on human behavior not econometric modeling. For Austrians, incentives matter. Austrians believe in Say's Law: supply creates it own demand.

The father of Austrian Economics is Karl Menger who taught at the University of Vienna in the 1870's. Authors in this field include von Mises, Hayek, Rothbard and Hazlett. Mises published *The Theory of Money and Credit* and *Human Action*. Hayek's *Road to Serfdom* remains well read among conservatives.

A second discipline is that of the Monetarists. Milton Friedman founded this school of thought at the University of Chicago. A Nobel Lauriat, Friedman's views can best be summed up by the phrase, "money matters." The monetarists were champions of free market economics and received credit for being the first to challenge the Keynesian School. Monetarists do not believe in a gold standard, but favor a fixed rate of monetary expansion. Freidman does an excellent job of explaining inflation as a monetary phenomenon.

Milton Friedman co-authored *A Monetary History of the United States 1867-1960* and is best known for his book *Capitalism and Freedom.* Nobel Lauriat Robert Mundell has authored many works that share similarities with the Monetarists.

Keynesian economics is the most widely accepted and most taught economic theory in Western civilization. John Maynard Keynes authored *The General Theory of Employment, Interest, and Money.* Published in 1936, this work gained immediate acceptance for government intervention in times of economic downturns. This philosophy espouses a fiscal role for stimulating aggregate demand in the economy. (It is understandable that this economic school is endearing to governments around the world). Keynes believed in a paradox of thrift: that savings is good for the individual, but bad for the nation. Keynes argued for inflation as a tactic to foster growth. Well known Keynesians include John Kenneth Galbraith, Paul Samuelson and Paul Krugman.

The seventeen principles follow and are divided into four sections each with its own thread of continuity.

ON ECONOMICS

1. All economics are microeconomics.

The big picture usually captures the headlines and the attention most times. Be it quarterly Gross Domestic Product (GDP) figures, money supply data, productivity or the producer price index, the larger players receive the most coverage. Economics, as a discipline, traces its origin to the Greek language, where economics is referred to as the management of the household.

It is the rational actor who is often "lumped" into the herd with graphs, regarding aggregate demand and supply. However, it is the actions of individuals that make an economy function.

Economics is not mathematics, it is psychology. Economics is about how actors respond to incentives.

2. Businesses do not pay taxes; consumers do.

It is a common misperception or ploy by politicians that government can increase taxes on business and not impact the entire economy. In reality, business does not own resources; households do and thus individuals bear the burden of all taxes.

Business is "where." It is where you work, drink coffee, have lunch, go to and return from. You cannot tax a "where." When business is taxed, it will shift costs, charging consumers more at the register, paying employees less or not increasing dividends to shareholders.

3. When you live beyond your means, you must do one or more of these three things:

Reduce savings
Borrow
Sell assets

The pronoun you refers to individuals, business and government. This concept is self explanatory.

4. When compared to a ship, the United States economy has three permanent anchors:

Taxation
Regulation
Litigation

All taxes depress economic growth, income and property taxes are the most damaging, not sales taxes, as commonly believed. Although seventy two percent of GDP is comprised of consumer demand, consumers really do not know what they want until they see it.

The government must create an atmosphere in which entrepreneurs and job creators will take risks. Savings is actually more important than spending, since saved assets are the surplus capital which will be borrowed and used for business expansion.

Overregulation costs the average citizen thousands of dollars in lost purchasing power.

Overzealous trial lawyers, especially those who target specific industries for huge actions, increase costs to all of us with insurance premiums rising every year. Many physicians spend in excess of $100,000 in medical malpractice insurance on an annual basis. Some in the OB-GYN field can spend in excess $175,000.

5. All economic behavior is based on your own self interest.
Adam Smith, *The Wealth of Nations*

We all do things to benefit ourselves. In economics, by being the best, companies are indirectly serving others. Companies who fail often make inferior products or cannot adapt to changing market conditions to meet the wants and needs of consumers. Successful companies grow because of their reputation, superior products and service.

6. Prices must be able to tell the truth.
Benjamin M. Anderson, *Economics and the Public Welfare*

Prices serve many purposes. They coordinate supply and demand; allocate scarce resources to their most highly valued use; provide an efficient guide to the use of resources; serve as a guide to future production and act as a signal.

When the government intervenes and artificially establishes a price, it creates a surplus or a shortage. This distorts markets and skews incentives.

It has been stated, "There is never a shortage of goods, only a shortage of prices."[1]

7. Long term growth is based on two main factors:

What you've got (inputs)
How you use it (usage)

Although this concept may be applied to concrete factors, it is most directed at the concept of human capital development or investment in people.

8. Inflation benefits those who receive money first, before prices rise.

When government creates money faster than the economy grows, inflation is the result. Whether money is created at the printing press or electronically through the ledgers in the banking system, the people who receive capital in the form of loans at the beginning of a business cycle are far better off than the people at the end of a business cycle when both prices of products and interest rates have increased.

ON BUSINESS

9. Business borrows first.

Capital is the core of capitalism. Prior to selling any products, the entrepreneur must take on risk in the form of borrowed assets. Financing is the key to any endeavor. Even at the most microeconomic level, very few individuals write a check when they buy their home. This is why national savings is more important than spending. Most economic theory is demand driven, with spending trumping savings. This is backward.

More emphasis must be placed on savings and capital formation by reducing or eliminating the capital gains tax. This is a tax most associated with purchasing an asset at a given price and selling at a higher price; the gain is subject to tax. It is not a tax on capital; it is a tax on the formation of capital. People should be encouraged to save as savings is postponed spending and allows others to borrow money.

Modern lending dates to the Venetians, who needed capital to finance the building of ships. It was difficult to pay for a ship, before fish were caught or goods were delivered to ports of call. Loans were needed to support ventures that had not yielded any profit. This is true today as no one generates sales without making an outlay of capital first. The capital comes in the form of a loan. Contrary to popular political belief, you do need bondholders to build cars.

10. First rule of business: maximize shareholder wealth (they take all of the risk).

Most wealth obtained in this nation has not been stolen or inherited. Wealth has been created by individuals selling a product or service in a market place where other individuals, by their own free will, perceived both value or use in this product and gladly paid what they believed was a reasonable price.

We, the free market, make successful suppliers and producers wealthy. It is usually done over years or decades. If a business owner makes a poor product, he or she will go out of business and could lose their house and potentially future income. Henry Ford experienced business failure twice before founding the Ford Motor Company.

At the end of the payroll period, if the business does poorly, the owner receives less compensation. If results are better than expected, then a reward is due, as it should be. The shareholder bears all of the risk.

ON TRADE

11. Sanctions never work.

Fidel Castro came to power when Dwight Eisenhower was President. The United States imposed sanctions on Cuba believing it would remove Castro. Since then, ten presidential administrations continued to embrace this strategy and Castro is still in power. Only recently did the Obama Administration signal an openness to begin more than just a casual dialog with our Caribbean neighbor. The best method to remove a totalitarian regime is though engagement, reaching the public through technology and reinforcing private property rights through trade and specialization.

Following the First Persian Gulf War, the United States and many allies imposed economic sanctions on Iraq. Sanctions had little impact on the regime, but resulted in mass suffering of the populace.

During the crisis in Bosnia, the United States and its allies imposed sanctions against Serbia. Inflation, according to some reports, rose 4,000%. The populace suffered, the leadership remained. It was not until American carrier based aircraft bombed the Serbs and their allies, that results were achieved.

12. Imports are just as important as exports.

We do not make everything in the United States. We never have and we never will. Imports provide choice, while keeping domestic producers honest. Imports promote efficiency and foster innovation. Imports allow for exports. Many imports are raw materials, vital to production of domestic goods. At the end of the day, trade is a good deal. We should not punish people who want to do business with us. Further, imports are necessary for comparative advantage to work, which makes us all better off.

My Father worked for 48 years with General Motors. He spent most of his career with Die Engineering at Fisher Body. Years ago he told me that the best thing that ever happened to GM was the Toyota Corolla. I asked, "Why?" He said that it forced GM to move to a front wheel drive with a transverse mounted engine and use lighter steel employing fewer workers. My dad was a member of the United Auto Workers.

ON GOVERNMENT

13. The free market has not failed, government has failed.

Many government regulations are designed to rein in the market, rather than promote it. The unenlightened benevolence of government is the source of many of the nation's ills. Roosevelt's New Deal helped prolong the Great Depression and increased the suffering on its citizens. In many instances, we succeed in spite of government, not because of it.

The New Deal misallocated scarce resources to produce items which would have normally not been built.

14. "When in doubt, do no harm."

The Hippocratic Oath doctors take is one which should be applied to government officials at all levels.

15. For every job created in the public sector, at least one is destroyed in the private sector.

Why? The market is the most efficient user of capital. It takes resources to support that job and capital is removed from the most efficient users and best decision makers, i.e. business and individuals to support government.

16. When the government spends money, it has received it from one of three sources:

Taxation
Borrowing
Creation

In order to start a business, expand or invest, business borrows first, as previously mentioned. Capital formation is critical. Taxation or borrowing by government takes money away from the most efficient users of capital, individuals and business. By its very nature, government is too far from information to make the most informed decisions on how to most efficiently use money.

The creation of excess money, either fiduciary credit or fiat, is inflationary. Expansion of the money stock at a rate greater than the economy grows produces inflation and ultimately weakens the currency.

17. Deficits matter.

The belief that the government can increase the deficit and the corresponding debt to an infinite level is so preposterous it almost defies description.

The dollar's strength is determined by many factors. First, among equals is the amount of money available or that will be made available. The government will have to repay bondholders and there is no indication that raising taxes will be sufficient to return the capital that has been provided. The only way to pay all of the debt is by issuing more debt, which is highly inflationary and will weaken the dollar. With the debt exceeding $11.4 trillion, there is reason to be concerned. Long term, this behavior is not only fiscally irresponsible; it weakens the domestic social order and the United States' standing among its global partners.

In June 2005, I asked Ed Meese, Ronald Reagan's Attorney General, about the national debt and both political parties understanding of its impact. He stated, "It's a fairly abstract concept in Washington."

These concepts, seventeen in total, one no more important than the other, represent the core concepts of this book. More than economic theory, they are based on the common sense needed most in our time. Some principles will appear more than once. The concept of where money comes from and the impact of taxation is referenced often.

Nine Key Elements for a Free Market

Related to these principles are nine key elements which are essential to the functioning of a successful free market economy.[2] The first three: free trade, stable currency and private property rights are the most important. These elements form the cornerstone on which a solid foundation from which economic growth is built. Free trade fosters innovation, competition and allows for mutually beneficial exchange to occur globally. Trade enhances comparative advantage. Stable currency permits society to conduct commerce which is not distorted by inflation, speculation or devaluation. Currency is a means of exchange and is not necessarily wealth; it allows wealth to be created. Private property rights provide ownership and incentive for citizens to retain what they earn. Private property rights help keep government power in check.

A functioning price system is distorted when a centralized body does not accept the price established by the market. In the 1970's, the Nixon Administration believed the price of oil was too high and the government established a lower price. This created a price ceiling and resulted in shortages as producers were reluctant to produce enough at a low price and consumers demanded too much oil at that price. The second distortion is known as a price floor. In this event, the government establishes a price too high and a surplus occurs. The most glaring example is crop subsidies. The farmers overproduce, redirecting scarce resources that would otherwise be used more efficiently.

A nation's division of labor increases its specialization. This element provided the answer to Adam Smith's question concerning what determined the wealth of a nation. How citizens spend their productive time results in profits and losses for companies and countries. It also contributes to Gross Domestic Product. As a society becomes more specialized, most actions take place without the populace having to think about what to do.

Market incentives, simply stated, give people a reason to get up in the morning. Higher rates of taxation, oppressive regulation and unfair legal systems inhibit incentives. If tax rates reach ninety percent, why bother working when you would have little to show for your effort? Human beings require motivation to do anything. The government's role is to provide an atmosphere in which success may occur.

The rule of law is vital to the functioning of a nation. It is important that an independent judiciary enforce laws and address grievances. Due process must be allowed and governments must not stymie access to the court. Rational adherence to the law by the vast majority of any society allows it to function in a manner consistent with the established principles of right and wrong. For the United States, the result is a culture which finds its bedrock in order and reason.

A free flow of ideas allows for growth, coordination and innovation. Censorship in totalitarian regimes inhibit thought and depresses positive ideas, often labeled as radical and considered a threat to the ruling authority. There is an enormous opportunity cost to censorship; citizens spend time in rebellion rather than making a country more developed. History is on the side of freedom and liberty.

A comment is required regarding the nation's political stability. An enormous amount of the world's mined gold supply is stored at the Federal Reserve Bank of New York and Ft. Knox, Kentucky. The gold of our adversaries is kept there, too. There is an implied trust that whatever happens, someone in the United States will ensure that these assets will be secured. This requires great faith and trust in our system, especially from those abroad.

On Friday, November 22, 1963, President John F. Kennedy died. An immediate debate ensued as to whether to play professional football on

Sunday. The leadership of the league decided to play and had a moment of silence. This reinforced to the world that the United States would remain in a status quo, despite the horrific slaying of the President.

The concept of political stability and not holding long term grudges, especially between rival tribes also makes the United States different from many other nations. I know from talking to U.S. Army officers that groups from Bosnia to Iraq still fight over disputed towns or territories from centuries past. We are fortunate that does not happen in our nation. Fights like these occur in American city council meetings and court rooms, not in violent clashes.

At the end of the Civil War, Robert E. Lee and other leaders of the south decided to surrender, rather than wage a protracted guerilla war that could have lasted for decades.[3] Many nations often mock the United States for a lack of history or culture, but we tend to move on. There is a lot to be said about that. In our country, every day is a new day.

When the outcome of the Bush v. Gore case remained in doubt, citizens went about their day to day affairs until the Supreme Court issued its verdict. No one worried; we went to work and waited to see who would become president. The Republican tribe did not wage war against the Democratic tribe. As the old saying goes, "Every society has to choose between lawyers and guns and we have chosen lawyers."

Taken together, these nine key elements complement the seventeen principles of economics to provide a solid foundation for sound economic policy.

Two columns appear to the right of the key elements. These are the government's policies that distort the element essential to the market's proper functioning. The column to the far right is the result of that distortion.

Table 2.1

Distortions of a Free Market Economy

Key Element	Distortion	Result
Free Trade	Quota/Tariff	Higher Prices/Fewer Choices Shortages
Stable Currency	Inflation	Devaluation/Higher Prices Speculation/Poverty
Private Property Rights	Taxation	Decrease Incentives/Leasing Renting
Price System	Floors/Ceilings	Surpluses/Shortages
Division of Labor	Unions/Guilds	Inhibit National Comparative Advantage/Formation of Labor Cartel/Job losses
Market Incentives	Taxation Regulation Litigation	Decrease economic growth Increase input & usage costs Increase insurance costs, etc.
Rule of Law	Too many laws	Too many lawyers, lawsuits Overcrowded legal system Higher insurance costs Lower economic growth
Free Flow of Ideas	Censorship	Slows Human Capital Development/High Opportunity Cost
Political Stability	No progression No continuity	Tyranny and servitude Inability to Plan Anarchy

The nine key elements listed above form the cornerstone for successful free market economies. The second order consequences of misguided actions serve as a warning to policymakers eager to curry favor with the public but ignorant of the results. Government has operated for decades on the premise by James Buchanan, that it could "concentrate the benefits and spread the costs." One can reasonably assume that the costs have now been borne by as many as are able.

The seventeen principles provide guidelines for legislators in the philosophy of how markets best function by applying commonsense factors to make policy. When these concepts are ignored or recklessly abandoned, major economic crises ensue.

CHAPTER 3
AN AVOIDABLE CATASTROPHE

The definition of insanity: Repeating the same behavior,
expecting a different outcome.

There is no single economic event during the past 100 years that has had such a major impact on the world at the time or influenced the discipline of economics as the Great Depression.

There is a general myth that perpetuates the world of academics that goes something like this: The "roaring '20s" were caused by greedy business speculating on the stock market. The market crashed in October 1929 due to the gold standard. Roosevelt's New Deal put everyone back to work and righted the economy and World War II ended the Great Depression. In fact, nothing could be further from the truth.

Although entire books have been devoted to the Great Depression, the intent in this work is to highlight the most important factors leading to and prolonging this tragic and avoidable event. The Great Depression was not caused by one single event, but rather by a series of poor government policies and ignorance of the consequences of actions. In short, an inability to comprehend and respect the basic laws of economics doomed the world to a dismal decade where ideas so perverse in nature were accepted as the norm. In the 1930's, radicals came to power when times were bad precisely because the average citizen accepted the worst ideas just because they sounded good and that the implementation of these policies would provide relief. In short, radicals provided the populace with hope. Many events set the stage for the onset of the Great Depression.

World War I actually set up the circumstances that led to the beginning of the Great Depression. It effectively ended the prosperity of the Age of Classical Liberalism, which lasted from 1815 to 1914. Empires collapsed, and the age of the gold standard, for all practical purposes ended. The great era of free trade, championed by the British, ended and would not resume until the 1990's. Millions died needlessly and the peace gained was only, "an Armistice for twenty years," as Ferdinand Foch so presciently stated in 1918.[1]

Harsh reparations against Germany set the stage for Hitler's rise to power. Forced to accept the brunt of the burden of blame for the war, the German Empire lost territory, rolling stock and owed millions of dollars in payments, largely to France. As Germany had abandoned gold as a means of currency regulation to print money to fund the war, the German Mark had grown worthless. In order to meet the demands of the allied powers and domestic budgets, Germany simply resorted to the printing press; resulting in hyperinflation. By February 1924, the exchange ratio of the mark was 4.58 trillion to $1.00.[2] Social unrest during the 1920's was common in Germany as socialists, fascists, communists and other factions vied for power.

Further adding to this global monetary instability was the inability of the British to properly reset the pound sterling to gold. During the war, the amount of money in circulation in Great Britain increased as the government expanded the money supply to pay for the war. They attempted to reestablish the relationship of their currency to gold at a specified price. This price or "peg" represented the pre-war levels in 1914. Having added millions of pounds over four years had, in effect, devalued the currency and the peg should have been set much lower. It may be of interest that the man who bears responsibility for this miscalculation was the Chancellor of the Exchequer, Great Britain's Treasury Secretary, Winston Churchill.[3]

This action set the stage for the newly created Federal Reserve (Fed) of the United States to add to the problem by weakening the dollar to support the pound. Statistics in money stock demonstrate that the Fed increased the money supply during the years of 1922, 1924 and 1925.[4] This not only helped offset the weakness of the pound but established the conditions for the post World War I boom in the United States known as the "roaring '20s." Lower rates and the infusion of capital helped infuse liquidity into the American banking system, beginning a decade long business cycle. There is also speculation that the Fed desired to keep interest rates low to avoid recessions in 1924 and 1928. (These were election years).

As the United States emerged from the war with its property intact, the 1920's became a decade of an economic boom. Rather than spending money on rebuilding and recovery, capital was directed at productive endeavors. The United States also began to develop as a major industrial power. Much of the working population began to leave the farms as early as the 1870's as the nation transitioned from a largely agricultural economy to one with a growing manufacturing base. The post war nation became more dependent on trade in order to obtain goods, which were produced more cheaply abroad. This also included agricultural products.

The markets showed improvements, as well. The Dow Jones Industrial Average rose throughout the decade. Spurred on by easy credit and lower margin requirements, more money poured into the equity markets.[5] Buying on margin allows investors to leverage, which works well when stocks are rising in price. However, in a declining market, where the value of the stock drops below the purchase price, the investor is subject to a "margin call." Simply explained, the brokerage firm requires that the investor deposit more cash to cover the loss of the stock. In a rapidly declining market, the customer may be forced to immediately pay all of his margin debt, plus interest.

By 1928, the conditions of the money stock and that of the booming equity market required a change of Fed policy. Further, pending inflation may have been anticipated. The Fed began to "tighten" by increasing interest rates. Globally, there appeared to be a growing concern about the availability of gold. Some academics believe that this growing monetary worry about gold's availability was self perpetuating. Others argue that the existence of a gold standard itself directly contributed to the "worldwide economic decline."[6]

A more important and ominous factor that would cause world-wide disruption was the election of Herbert Hoover in 1928 and the emergence of the Smoot Hawley Tariff Bill in congress. Hoover ran largely as a protectionist and the Republicans desired to assist the American farmer from the adverse effects of cheap imports.[7]

Opponents of free trade and political opportunists favored a tariff. A tariff would restrict imports by making them more expensive and, in theory, simply correct the trade imbalance. As in Adam Smith's time, trade was viewed as a zero sum game. Congress had no understanding of the adverse affects of a tariff on American consumers, trade relations with our neighbors or the capital markets. Further, many lawmakers failed to realize the effects of international retaliation on American companies, which relied on open access to foreign markets to thrive.

Tariffs are a tax on goods and services, which cross international borders. Tariffs raise the price of imports by a specified amount. The unintended consequence of the tariff is to raise the price of domestic goods which compete with the import. Incidentally, prices of domestic goods will remain high, even if some of the imports are exempted from the tariff. Tariffs cause prices to rise, create shortages and decrease the net income of corporations. Perceived lower earnings, either now or in the future, will cause stock prices to decrease in value immediately.

How markets work can best be explained from Jude Wanniski's, *The Way the World Works*.

> The market is the most accurately programmed computer on the planet, the closest expression of the mind of the electorate itself. It places a value on each company within it, based on its calculation of that company's *future* income stream…The most important information coming to the market is political news. War and peace can turn the chemistry of a single mind. Political news is volatile, because it can instantly and dramatically alter the market's future income streams.[8]

In Chapter 7, the "Stock Market and the Wedge," Wanniski brilliantly traces the major news of the tariff bill as it moved through congress and compares it to the returns of the Dow Jones Industrial Average. This step by step analysis is accompanied by critiques of other economists' views on the crash.[9] All ignore the effects of tariffs on the future income streams of corporations and the present value of stocks. Tariffs raise prices and create shortages. A tariff is an international tax, which someone must pay.

Although the market began to show signs of weakness on "black Thursday," October 24, 1929, the news that tanked the market was made public on Sunday, October 27th. At a meeting in Philadelphia, Senator Reed stated in an address that the tariff bill could die in the present session of congress.[10]

However, in Washington, Senator Smoot, the bill's primary sponsor, made it quite clear that if the tariff bill did not pass in the current session of Congress it would go on to the next session. Even Senator Simmons, leader of the Democratic forces, said that for the bill to die, "the Republican Party would have to kill it." He continued, "The bill cannot die until a majority of the Senate says so."[11] The Democrats intended to see that Hoover's plan to relieve agriculture would be carried out.

On Monday October 28th, the front page of *The New York Times*, carried the news, but the story appeared mid-page to a minor column header entitled, "Leaders Insist Tariff Will Pass."[12] Further, when Tuesday's headlines detailed the crash itself, the paper did not link the crash to the certainty of the tariff's passage or the potential impact on future earnings of domestic or international corporations whose stock prices plummeted. No one at that time understood that the tariff could so directly and immediately impact the market. Not many understand it today.

The Federal Reserve Bank of Dallas 2002 Annual Report sums it up best.

> The stock market hates protectionism. That lesson-perhaps the clearest history has ever taught-comes from the Smoot-Hawley Tariff Act of 1930. In the late 1920's farmers, whose economic fortunes had not kept with industrialists', lobbied Congress for tariffs on agricultural products. The proposed act had few political sponsors at first (two of the three major political parties opposed it), and the stock market ignored it.
>
> But as word of the bill spread, more and more U.S. producers joined the bandwagon, arguing for tariffs to assist domestic industry or protect them from foreign competition. Smoot-Hawley eventually expanded to cover more than 20,000 items across the gamut of U.S. production, with rates practically prohibitive to trade. With so many political constituents now on board, the Progressive and Democratic parties jumped the fence and on October 28, 1929, joined the Old Guard Republicans in supporting the legislation. That day, the stock market crashed, falling 12 percent.
>
> In the months that followed, foreign governments filed 34 formal protests, and 1,028 economists petitioned President Hoover not to sign the bill, but he did, on June 17, 1930, and the Great Depression engulfed the nation. The Dow Jones Industrial Average fell from a daily high of 381 in September 1929 to a low of 41 in 1932 as world trade contracted from $5.7 billion to just $1.9 billion three and a half years later.
>
> It was the most important lesson markets ever taught: Protect and destroy.[13]

The market reaction to the decrease in future earnings is shown in comparison to the decrease in global trade.[14]

Figure 3.1

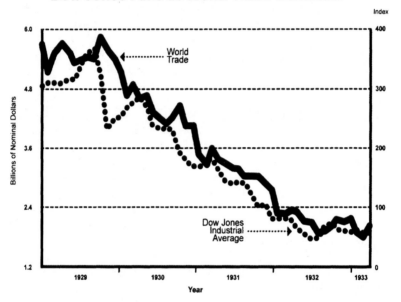

If the projected corporate growth rate or dividends decrease, the present value of a company stock will be less. If the cost of goods used to produce a product increases, the anticipated future earnings of the company will drop accordingly and the present value of the stock will be adjusted to reflect the loss of net income. This is a very simple calculation performed by rational actors in the market every second.

Although the tariff bill did not become law until June 17, 1930, the market discounted future earnings and adjusted the present value of the underlying securities of all corporations once it was convinced that the action was certain. In short, the market expressed a collective expectation of decreased earnings and tanked. This was a very rational correction.

Table 3.1 lists fourteen major product categories with the comparison to the Tariff Act of 1922 and the Tariff Act of 1930. These items are listed as percentage with duties computed using the 1928 value and volume of imports.[15]

Table 3.1

Selected Tariff Increases

Product Category	Act of 1922	Act of 1930
1. Chemicals, Oils, Paint	28.92%	36.09%
2. Earthenware & Glassware	45.52	53.73
3. Metals	33.71	35.08
4. Sugar, Molasses	67.85	77.21
5. Tobacco	63.09	64.78
6. Agricultural Products	22.37	35.07
7. Alcoholic Beverages	36.48	47.44
8. Cotton	40.27	46.42
9. Flax, Hemp, Jute	18.16	19.14
10. Wool	49.54	59.83
11. Silk	56.56	59.13
12. Rayon	52.68	53.62
13. Papers and Books	24.51	26.06
14. Sundries	20.99	28.45

Once the tariff bill became law other nations retaliated. Great Britain passed the Import Duties Act in 1932, the first general tariff law in more than 100 years. Part II of this law raised tariffs on American imports by 100 percent.[16] Spain increased tariffs on American cars by 150 percent. Sales of these autos dropped ninety percent. Italy raised tariffs on U.S. radios by 500 percent.[17] By 1934, France restricted the import of more than 3,000 goods with quotas. We infuriated our Canadian neighbors by imposing tariffs on everything from halibut to milk to lumber. We imposed tariffs on Swiss watches. An editorial ran in the Swiss paper asking basically everyone in the country to boycott all American goods.[18]

Perhaps the least known but most severe action occurred when, by 1935, thirty four American trading partners imposed exchange controls on their citizens restricting their ability to obtain foreign currency for travel or trade. The list included: Argentina, Brazil, China, Germany, Greece, Hungary, Japan, Mexico, Poland, Rumania and Yugoslavia. Globally, exchange controls had not been imposed in this magnitude in 400 years.[19]

Sumner Welles, FDR's undersecretary of state mused that Smoot Hawley helped the German government bring about an '"autarchic economic policy, which in turn was a contributing factor in bringing about the Second World War.'"[20] Most historians and economists agree that economic nationalism was the root cause of World War II. The old adage proved true: when goods cannot cross borders, armies will.

The net effect of the tariff bill was to drop American export trade back to the monthly sustained levels of February 1905.[21] U.S. imports decreased to July 1905 levels.[22]

Table 3.2

US Export/Import Data

Month	Year	U.S. Exports	
February	1905	$106,900,000	
October	1928	550,000,000	
February	1933	101,500,000	
October	*1941*	*$666,400,000*	*Recovery from 1928 levels*

Month	Year	U.S. Imports	
July	1905	$ 84,500,000	
April	1929	410,700,000	
July	1932	79,400,000	
July	*1946*	*$434,800,000*	*Recovery from 1929 levels*

The reason exports improved before imports is most likely due to the lend lease program to Great Britain and other allies. The United States' homeland remained intact, as many of our trading partners had their infrastructure completely destroyed and millions of its citizens killed, so imports from these pre-war trading partners lagged for years.

The average volume of world trade decreased from a monthly average of $2.9 billion in 1929 to $1 billion in 1933.[23] This tariff raised the duty on more than 25,000 imports into the United States.[24] According to the U.S. Department of State, between 1929 and 1934 global trade declined sixty six percent.[25]

The chart below is trade data from a different source, which illustrates annual global trade, spiraling downward from a peak in 1929 of $5.3 billion to a low of $1.8 billion by 1933.[26]

Figure 3.2

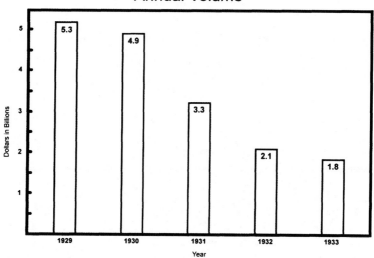

World Trade Implodes
1929 - 1933
Annual Volume

It is ironic that the Tariff Act of 1930 had as its aim, "To regulate commerce with foreign countries, to encourage the industries of the United States, to protect American labor, and for other purposes."[27] The impact was precisely the opposite. Far from regulating commerce with other nations, the tariff act prevented commerce from occurring. The price of imports, which were purchased voluntarily by American consumers, soared. Industries were immediately affected by higher costs and an inability to export. Shortages occurred. Far from protecting American labor, millions became unemployed, not only in the United States, but worldwide. The Tariff Act was an unmitigated disaster.

Most presidents only make one major mistake while in office. Herbert Hoover made two. If disrupting the trading lanes and tanking the markets were not enough, Hoover managed to convince congress to increase taxes, in some cases over 70 percent, by passing the Revenue Act of 1932 into law. Hoover's desire to balance the budget by raising taxes deprived business of its retained earnings that could have provided the means to an economic recovery.[28]

An Avoidable Catastrophe

Table 3.3

Internal Revenue Receipts
Years ending June 30, 1929-1935
(In thousands of dollars)

Year	Revenue
1935	$3,227,690
1934	2,640,604
1933	1,604,424
1932	1,561,006
1931	2,429,781
1930	3,039,295
1929	2,938,019

The states also raised taxes, making the business of job creation and economic expansion even more difficult. Sixteen states began to tax personal income, fifteen states taxed corporations. In 1930, state tax revenues totaled $2.1 billion. By 1940, they had reached $4.1 billion, nearly doubling.[29]

Adding to this economic contraction, the money supply actually decreased by one third from 1929 to 1933.[30] The stock market contracted and the prices of most assets fell, caused by too much supply and not enough demand. Many consumers were wiped out. With tariffs in place, increased taxes, banks not willing to lend, consumers not able to borrow and a collapsed market, the depression was well under way.

Roosevelt offered hope to a battered nation and was elected on his New Deal policies. Although many attribute these policies to Roosevelt's administration, many programs were actually begun by Hoover.[31]

The National Industrial Recovery Act of 1933 allowed for the creation of its enforcement agency, The National Recovery Administration, (NRA). This body received the unflattering nickname the "National Run Around."[32] This act mandated fixed prices and lowered output. Many of Roosevelt's cronies believed that the depression was caused by decreasing wages. The solution was to simply mandate that business pay higher wages to workers and the depression would end.[33] The NRA allowed labor unions the ability to draft codes forcing industry to pay above market wages.[34] The NRA had 1,400 "compliance enforcers from 54 state and branch offices."[35] They had the authority to levy fines and issue jail terms. The agency acted with malice toward job creators and supported unions over business, further hindering economic growth.

> The precise components of macaroni were specified. NRA codes prohibited consumers from picking their own chickens in the poultry markets. In one particularly egregious example, a dry cleaner was thrown in jail for three months for charging 35 cents to press a suit (the minimum price was 40 cents).[36]

In the summer of his first year in office, President Roosevelt torpedoed the World Economic Conference. The sole purpose of this meeting in London was to reopen the dialogue between nations regarding currency issues.[37] The conference began on June 12, 1933. Sixty four nations attended. There were three general positions at the conference. The French favored gold, the Americans favored floating rates and a policy of domestic inflation; the British favored a combination of the two.[38] Discussions ensued with a potential compromise reached at the end of June.

On July 3rd, Roosevelt issued the "bombshell message," named because of the impact on the conference. In sum, the President rejected the idea of an international monetary agreement based on gold or international compromise.[39] The conference continued for a few more weeks without result. Had there been a resolution of currency issues and further discussion on trade, world history may have been altered. Instead, FDR turned inward for revenue to fund government programs.

Roosevelt raised taxes with more vigor than Hoover. FDR signed the Revenue Acts of 1934, 1935, and 1936. All these increases deprived business of needed capital and individuals of their disposable personal income. Roosevelt tripled taxes from $1.6 billion in 1933 to $5.3 billion in 1940.[40] With less incentive to work why make the effort?

In 1935, FDR raised the highest marginal tax rate to 79 percent. He later raised it to 90 percent.[41]

Roosevelt blamed gold for the depression and outlawed its holding by private citizens. The government confiscated millions of dollars worth of gold from the public.[42] Had an individual done this to another citizen, he would have been arrested and thrown in jail. Roosevelt deprived people of their private property. Where was the rule of law?

Because agriculture was an important export of the United States, as well as an import, farms failed because of an inability to get crops to market. Farmers who had lobbied for years to enact Smoot Hawley watched their exports decrease from a pre-Smoot Hawley level in 1929 of $1.8 billion to $590 million in 1933.[43] In 1930, 21.5 percent of America's work force was employed in agriculture, with this sector of the economy comprising 7.7% of GDP.[44]

Further, since America's banks were largely confined to one local region or city, they were not well diversified regarding populace or industries. In general, as the local economy went so went the local banks. With rural banks so dependent on farms, when the farms failed, so did the banks.

FDR passed the Wagner Act of 1935, establishing the National Labor Relations Board.[45] This body, made up of pro-union, anti-business appointees, made it very difficult for business to get a "fair shake." Further, an argument can be made that this board violated the due process clause of the 5th and 14th Amendments to the U.S. Constitution as it places the power of judge, jury and executioner in the hands of an unelected body, with little or no recourse for business. It removed the judicial branch of government from the trial process. Why should business be subject to a "special process," without benefit of a jury by its peers, rather by its adversaries?

Roosevelt added insult to injury with the passage of The Fair Labor Standards Act of 1938 creating the minimum wage.[46] This type of economic distortion is known as a price floor, which creates too much supply of a given good, in this case, labor and not enough demand for labor by employers. A price floor creates a surplus and results in higher rates of unemployment. Roosevelt's desire to force business to hire workers actually made business less likely to hire, harming the people the President desired to help.

Roosevelt's "make work" projects resulted in an increase in the national debt. From June 1933 to June 1938, the debt increased from $22.538 billion to $37.164 billion; an increase of 60 percent.[47] Unemployment did not change as much as supporters of the New Deal may wish to admit. In 1933, unemployment stood at 12.83 million, by 1938 it was 10.39 million.[48] Clearly, this was Roosevelt's depression. It is interesting that despite much factual information concerning all of the mistakes that FDR made, he is still incorrectly held among scholars as a great president.[49]

Some argue that the economy improved after Roosevelt took office, but cannot explain the fact that unemployment remained high.[50] If the economy truly improved, jobs would have been created. The Roosevelt Administration had such contempt for business made it difficult for business to succeed. In fact, what little progress that was made in the 1930's was made in spite of the Roosevelt Administration, not because of it. The free market did not fail; the government failed.

In May 1939, Treasury Secretary Henry Morgenthau commented that the New Deal programs had failed.

> "We tried spending money. We are spending more than we have ever spent before and it does not work. . . We have never made good on our promises. . . I say after eight years of this Administration we have just as much unemployment as when we started. . . And an enormous debt to boot!"[51]

Further, as the false stimulus of credit expansion ended, the S&P 500 dropped sixty percent from March 6, 1937 to April 29, 1942.[52] Economic news did not cause the market to bottom. Most likely, it was the results from the Pacific Theater that signaled a turning point in the war. On April 18, 1942, James Doolittle led the raid on Tokyo, which caused minor damage, but greatly improved American morale. In early May, the U.S. engaged the Japanese at the Battle of the Coral Sea, effectively halting Japan's southwestward advance toward the Indian Ocean. In early June, the U.S. won a decisive battle at Midway, sinking four Japanese carriers. From that point onward, Japan would be on the defensive in the Pacific.

World War II did not end the depression. Roughly fifty million people died and many millions were injured both physically and psychologically, never to recover. Private property losses were immeasurable. Most of Europe, Japan and the western Soviet Union lay in ruins. Following the German surrender in May 1945, General Eisenhower traveled from his headquarters in Rheims, France to Moscow and remarked that he did not see one building left undamaged.[53] Contrary to some economic theory, wars are not good for the economy, as they are inherently destructive not constructive.

Roughly half of all the goods produced from 1939 to 1945 were destroyed in the war. In the United States, the work week increased from 40 to 48 hours.[54] The standard of living decreased. Rationing was commonplace throughout the world as critical and non-critical items were sent to the front. Meat, shoes and cheese were rationed.[55] Coffee, sugar, nylons and chocolate were among scarce items in the United States. Wage and price controls were established, distorting signals to consumers and producers. Automobiles and pleasure boats were not produced. Most industries switched to "war work." Shortages of goods occurred daily and some items disappeared from the shelves altogether, not to be seen until after the war's end. By September 30, 1945, the U.S. budget deficit reached 42.6 percent of GDP.[56]

The Great Depression ended because of the adoption of three major policies: currency stabilization, lifting of wage and price controls and reopening of the trading lanes.

In July 1944, the allied powers held an international monetary conference at Bretton Woods, New Hampshire in order to "lay the foundation for the post-war resurgence of trade."[57] Bretton Woods stabilized the currency at $35 per ounce of gold.[58] Modern day economists ridicule such an idea, but the gold provides a stable benchmark. Gold's price also provides a needed signal of inflation when central banks create too much money. Further, gold provides the market confidence that the underlying currency is sound. Gold imposes discipline.

Blaming the gold standard for causing the Great Depression is like looking at a puddle believing it is causing the rain.[59] This was a depression brought on by the collapse of trade that resulted in falling equity prices and the general collapse of the price system. There were more sellers than buyers. The so called "recovery" between 1933 and 1937 was temporary, caused by an artificial stimulus, not long lasting job creation and wealth. Unemployment only began decreasing later as the nation geared for war with millions entering the ranks of the armed forces and many laborers hired to produce arms and vehicles.

In 1946, President Truman lifted wage and price controls. The free market began to function.[60] When the government establishes price controls, markets become rigid. Prices must be able to tell the truth and adjust.[61]

Prices provide needed functions in an economy. They coordinate supply and demand. Prices channel scarce resources to their most highly valued use. They provide an efficient guide to the use of resources. Prices help determine future production. Most importantly, prices are a signal to producers and consumers. There is never a shortage of goods, only a shortage of prices.

In 1947, The General Agreement on Tariffs and Trade (GATT) provided the framework to reopen the trading lanes that the Smoot Hawley Tariff closed.[62] Although the Reciprocal Trade Agreements of 1934 did assist in lowering tariffs in a bi-lateral manner, nothing is a substitute for a global trade agreement. GATT also created the "most favored nation" status. Trade increases earnings and earnings drive markets. The Dow Jones Industrial Average took twenty five years to reach its level obtained in 1929. Severely wounded by the lack of global trade, a depression and a world war, the market finally regained its footing during the Eisenhower Administration.

History owes a debt of gratitude to President Harry Truman. His easing of market restrictions, wage and price controls, as well as allowing GATT to be implemented signified a marked policy reversal from FDR. This new approach may have signaled to the markets that the United States was, once again, open for business. Overseas there was good news as well.

In June 1948, in West Germany, a little known economist named Ludwig Erhard established the West German Mark and lifted wage and price controls, against the wishes of the allied occupying powers.[63] Although the Marshall Plan gets the lion's share of credit for restoring Western Europe's economy, the German economic miracle could not have occurred without the wisdom of Ludwig Erhard.

There are three real catastrophes that the Great Depression imposed upon mankind. The first was the immediate effects on the world at the time. The series of events and poor policy choices made by the American government certainly bear some of the blame for the creating the despair of the 1930's. In this decade, individuals came to power because their radical and ignorant ideas were accepted. In times of prosperity, these ideas would have been dismissed.

The second factor is the inflationary bias that economists and interventionists at the Federal Reserve believe should be permanent policy. These individuals view any deflation as bad, since deflation occurred in the depression. They don't realize that the collapse of asset prices was due to a rational decrease in stock prices, as the market adjusted for the anticipated loss of future earnings. Hence, today's "experts" argue for monetary stimulus, which weakens the currency, in order to battle deflation, which is a naturally occurring and positive consequence of competition in free global markets.

The third tragedy comprises a vast misunderstanding of the secondary consequences of government action. There is a common belief that in times of economic recession or duress, the government's role is to intervene to provide stimulus to the economy. Actually, it is the worst action a government can take. A recession is the market's method of correcting for overexpansion. It is not part of a cyclical problem; it is part of the solution. As of this writing, the Obama Administration is undertaking a massive fiscal stimulus along with additional Federal Reserve actions that can only complicate the recovery and further distort markets and the economy. New Deal policies and philosophies still live on seventy years after they failed in the 1930's.

Many of the hardships and damage from the Great Depression could have been prevented. Had common sense, prudent foreign policy and monetary stability carried the day, a recession in 1929 may have ended in 1930. Instead, the United States government waged a trade war against its neighbors, destroyed billions of dollars in global wealth and raised taxes on its own populace. The Roosevelt Administration had an opportunity to alleviate much of this suffering at the Global Economic Conference in the summer of 1933, but instead withdrew American support and proceeded on a path the led us to war.

The most important lesson learned from the Great Depression is that the United States must work diligently to keep the global trading lanes open. Protectionism leads to retaliation and increases economic nationalism. Unfortunately, as we open a new millennium, America risks further alienating its trading partners by following identical behavior that led us into the Second World War nearly seventy years ago.

CHAPTER 4
TRADE IS A GOOD DEAL

"My prosperity is dependent on the
prosperity of my neighbor."
Paul D. Ballew

Politicians, business and industry leaders are poised to choose whether we will, collectively, enjoy another Age of Classical Liberalism where enlightened ideas allowed for economic growth from 1815 to 1914, or move into what has been referred to the Age of Mercantilism. From 1500 to 1815 nations erected trading barriers and the rule of the game was "beggar thy neighbor" or "I can sell goods to your country, but you cannot sell goods to my country." Merchant and craft guilds impeded the division of labor. During this age, the wealth of a nation was erroneously determined by the amount of gold one possessed.

In any discussion of economics, one must begin with trade. Trade is the starting point; it is the foundation of all prosperity. "Trade allows nations to rise above the level of economic self sufficiency." [1] Trade occurs between individuals just as it does between nations. On a daily basis we trade our specialties for someone else's.

We conduct trade because we need to. Trade works, it has stood the test of time. It fulfills the needs of nations and individuals. Trade allows for diversity and an expansion of global knowledge, skills and innovation. Trade fosters efficiency and competition. Trade creates global partnerships and trust between nations. Trade is a voluntary process, it is mutually beneficial and trade is a good deal.

The Nobel Lauriat Milton Friedman's views on wealth and spare time are a testament to trade.

The chief characteristic of progress and development over the past century is that it has freed the masses from backbreaking toil and has

made available to them products and services that were formally mo-
nopolies of the upper classes, without any corresponding way expanding the products and services available to the wealthy.[2]

This has been made possible by specialization, which trade positive-
ly affects. The world emerged from the darkness of the Medieval or
Feudal Age because of the reemergence of trade between nation states
and the dismemberment of the guild system, which controlled the production and distribution of goods. Today's unions are similar to the
guilds of long ago. Although the proponents of organized labor profess
the benefits, the downside to unions for all nations is that unions impede
countries from naturally moving to their comparative advantage and fully
achieving specialization in a global economy.

The foundation of free trade in the United States can be found in the
Constitution. Article I, Section 9, establishes free trade between the
states. Not since the Roman Republic had such a large contiguous area
been subject to such free movement of commerce. The Articles of Con-
federation allowed for taxation of interstate goods and the economy un-
derperformed as a result. The Constitution corrected this.

The founding fathers got it right:

> No Tax or Duty shall be laid on Articles exported from any State. No
> Preference shall be given by any Regulation of Commerce or revenue
> to the Ports of one State over those of another; nor shall vessels
> bound to, or from, one State, be obliged to enter, clear, or pay duties
> in another.[3]

We clearly see the influence of Adam Smith here, even though there
is no reference. His book, *The Wealth of Nations* was widely read by
those individuals who were considered enlightened at the time and influenced the framers of the Constitution, even though Smith has received
little credit in the history books for this vital inclusion.

The United States adopted internal free trade, but still relied on tariffs and duties to fund most government operations until the early part of
the twentieth century when we adopted the income tax. Following the
repeal of the Corn Laws in 1846, Great Britain set the example as a free
trading nation. With the Royal Navy protecting the sea lanes against pi-
rates and other aggressors, commerce and prosperity ensued and the
United States benefited greatly from trade relations with its mother country. America turned its attention to internal growth without foreign wars
and other distractions which could have drained the nation's treasury and

its human capital. During the early part of the nineteenth century, the United States could have been categorized as an emerging market.

It was only in the twentieth century that United States' road to free trade began. One year following the collapse of the Global Economic Conference in London in July 1933, the United States signed the Reciprocal Trade Agreements Act in 1934. GATT and many other initiatives reduced tariffs over the next six decades. The principal reason for free trade: peace. The most consequential trade decision of the past 100 years was the Smoot-Hawley Tariff of 1930. Its passage increased economic nationalism, a root cause of the Second World War. International trade and taxation policies influence corporate and individual decisions on a daily basis. An example of this occurred with one of America's most distinguished film producers.

In 1997, Steven Spielberg went to France to begin looking at locations to film the D-Day landings for his new film "Saving Private Ryan." Instead of shooting a majority of the film in France, he only filmed the beginning and end of the film at the American military cemetery in Normandy. The reason: taxes. During an interview with the French in Deauville at the film's preview the next year, he stated that, "I wanted to shoot the entire film in France and came here first, but when our production team came here they found the taxes were 52%."[4] The additional taxes would have increased the cost of the film from $65 million to $95 million. Spielberg chose Ireland as the location instead, as the Irish government provided DreamWorks SKG with a tax break.[5] This policy by France actually cost the local economy millions in lost revenue and went against the grain of post World War II improvements in trade relations.

There are three major global trends that have emerged since 1945: falling political barriers, increased technological development and increased trade. Globally, prices are being forced downward. Falling political barriers provides an "opening" of societies to embrace capitalism and free trade by a free exchange of ideas. This trend has continued basically unabated, save the 1970's when more nations fell under communism than were liberated or achieved freedom.

Increased technological development allows for improvements in efficiency, which in turn increases productivity (more output for less input). Efficiency improves the production process so higher quality goods can be produced at a lower cost. This benefits consumers. Long term, efficiency creates better jobs for highly skilled workers. Short term, technology results in job losses as capital improvements shift labor from lower skilled jobs to fewer higher skilled jobs. This is known as the Ricardo Effect as business replaces labor with capital. Increased technological advances result in job losses. That being said, society clearly benefited from the railroad, even though operators of horse drawn wagons were adversely affected.

Increased trade provides the participants with greater choices and fosters innovation, through increased competition. We conduct trade because we need to. No one has ever made everything that they need or want and no one ever will. Globally, all consumers benefit from purchasing the best possible product at the lowest possible price. Even Plato and Aristotle spoke about the need for trade and exchange as it fostered specialization.

Trade is an evolutionary process, not a revolutionary one. Free markets and free societies evolve over time. Command based systems, such as communist regimes require a revolution to achieve change. Many individuals and institutions had been led to believe that the globalization occurred overnight. This is not true. From 1914 until 1989, international commerce was interrupted by World War I, the Great Depression, World War II and the Cold War. Globalization is reestablishing trading patterns that existed before 1914. Globalization is not a result of economics; it is a byproduct of the political process, which forced the collapse of communism.

There was profound progress in the world between 1980 and 1990. Much credit is correctly afforded to the Reagan Administration in taking on the task of directly confronting the Soviets with a renewed alliance with the British and Western Europeans. This was a direct reversal of détente, or peaceful cooperation, the failed strategy of the 1970's. Reagan forged alliances with Margaret Thatcher, Pope John Paul II and Solidarity in Poland. He championed the NATO defense buildup. Reagan offered direct aid in Grenada, Afghanistan and Central America to demonstrate resolve to the Soviets that the United States would act aggressively to defend its interests and its treaty obligations with its allies. These actions certainly pushed communism to the tipping point.

In the 1980's, technology had become more available, even behind the Iron Curtain. As the United States led the world economy out of the deep malaise of the 1970's, Eastern European nations still lagged behind their Western peers. Much of the developed world had access to global media such as the Voice of America, BBC and CNN. Many disenfranchised Eastern Bloc members, especially the youth, were able to view differences in the utopia of the communist state and the realities of the West. Nowhere was this more evident than in East and West Germany.

A peek across the fence separating these two nations spoke of a stark reality: the communist system had failed to deliver the goods. The Soviets and the occupied nations of Eastern Europe had poor centralized planning, terrible infrastructure, distorted employment levels and in some cases, currencies which could not be converted. In 1989, in East Germany, anger and protests grew. President Gorbachev could not roll the Red Army into East Germany as the Soviets did in the 1950's; the entire world was watching. Having lost a terribly conducted war in Afghanistan and with troubles at home, the Soviet Union was economically collapsing inward. The writing was on the wall, literally, as the landscape of Eastern Europe changed due to a new political reality and a resurgent force: liberty. As the Berlin Wall fell and the Iron Curtain succumbed, the world reestablished trade relations that had existed prior to World War I.

The evolutionary process of greater free trade continued. Combined with increased technological development and falling political barriers two other forces have emerged: increased resource mobility and decreased transaction costs.

Increased resource mobility allows businesses, individuals and capital to move globally. Two trillion dollars moves through the international financial markets every single day. That amounts to one seventh of U.S. annual GDP. This mobility allows for freedom as well. If a business climate is difficult in one county or state, the business owner will move elsewhere. If a nation does not create an environment that encourages the entrepreneur to take risks, jobs will move offshore. Business owners that leave to create jobs elsewhere are not traitors, they are survivors.

A recent example of this force in action occurred on June 3, 2009, when Steven Ballmer, CEO of Microsoft and other industry leaders met with senior members of the Obama Administration and congressional committees to warn them of the immediate consequences of changing corporate tax structure. The Administration wanted to limit expense deductions for certain foreign profits. Ballmer stated in an interview that Microsoft would move "lots of people out of the U.S."[6] In a global economy, there are many alternatives, should government increase the cost of doing business. American workers are the most adversely affected.

Decreased transaction costs result from increased global competition. Lower prices benefit consumers and force producers to make a better product at a lower price. Global competition can be intense for producers. Paul Cook from Munder Capital Management said it best, "In a global economy, you are only as profitable as your least sane competitor."[7] In this type of environment, deflationary forces are the norm and should be embraced. There are other positive factors at work globally.

The diagram that follows illustrates four major elements that foster successful development in an economy: stable macroeconomics, competitive microeconomics, human capital development and global linkages. Of these four, global linkages (trade) are often the most neglected. It is done at great opportunity cost as this element fosters competition, innovation, choice and an exchange of ideas.[8]

Figure 4.1

Economic Development Model

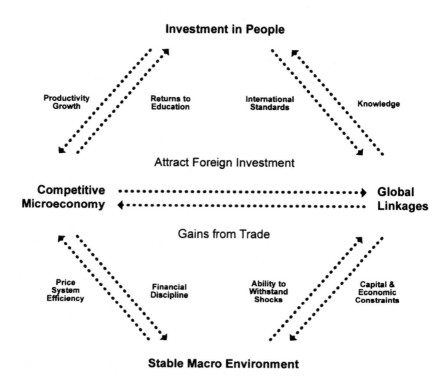

© Federal Reserve Bank of Chicago

Regarding gains from trade, there is a common misconception that if imports do not equal exports that this is bad for the United States. Actually, this means that Americans have more choices than anyone else in the world and consumers are allowed to shop globally for the best goods and services at the lowest possible price. Global competition and imports keep prices lower. Trade does not raise prices. It keeps them in check and places pressure on domestic producers to make a better product. Trade is deflationary in nature. The "trade deficit" does not produce inflation.

In measuring global trade there is a misuse of the word deficit. The international balance of payments is measured on a balance sheet not an income statement. Unlike the federal deficit, which is measured on an income statement, it is not numerically possible to have a deficit on a balance sheet. It is by nature balanced. In the case of trade, everything that is imported is already paid for. Throughout the United States, there are no IOU signs on anyone's television set manufactured in Japan or no bill past due hanging from articles of clothing made in Mexico. As most Americans have not had accounting courses, a brief explanation of the balance sheet and its history is appropriate. This business statement has been used for centuries.

In the fifteenth century, Luca Pacioli, the "forgotten genius" of the Renaissance, developed the system of double entry book keeping.[9] This system of debits and credits allows for a more dynamic financial picture, than just the use of basic revenue versus expenses calculation provided by an income statement. Debits and credits form the basis of modern accounting. This development is as important as the use of Arabic zero, which revolutionized mathematics, as the Roman system did not have the null form. Accounting helped the Renaissance progress and new accounting techniques were used immediately. Even Ferdinand and Isabella considered bookkeeping so important that they sent an accountant with Columbus on his first voyage.[10]

The trade deficit is difficult for most Americans to understand because they confuse this misnomer for an actual deficit, which is a problem. Here is an example of a deficit using an income statement.

The federal budget deficit occurs when the government spends more than it receives. If the government receives $1 trillion in revenue and spends $3 trillion, it has a deficit of $2 trillion. Examples of revenue are taxes, tariffs, fines or user fees. Government spending or expenses occur in the form of federal programs, subsidies, or salaries. A deficit occurs when expenses exceed revenue. The national debt is the cumulative value of all of the deficits with interest, which accrues daily.

The federal deficit is financed by selling securities, such as treasury bonds, to the public or foreigners, who finance the deficit in exchange for interest payments and the return of their principal. This is in contrast to the "trade deficit," that is a balance sheet transaction, which requires nothing to occur after the purchase or sale of the good or service. No one is owed anything.

The income statement and balance sheet provide the most basic information which forms the foundation of all accounting for business and government. However, one must not be confused with the other.

Much attention by politicians and economists continually focus on the trade deficit. Points are often made that the trade imbalance weakens the currency and it should be corrected. Although some merit can be made about an accumulation of dollars abroad, that may be returned to the United States, a far greater danger to the currency is the unrestrained creation of dollars by the Federal Reserve and the Treasury. Trade does not weaken the dollar; too many dollars weakens the dollar.

A weak dollar does not slow imports. It simply raises the price of goods that are not made here. Research shows a $58.2 billion difference between imports and exports in January 2008. The difference is 2003 was roughly $38 billion.[11] Despite assurance that a weak dollar would correct the imbalance, we continued to import more than we export; we simply paid a higher price for the same product as more dollars were required by the foreign supplier. This is especially true for oil.

There have been two major negative instances where the United States has attempted to correct the so called trade deficit. In 1928, the intent of the Smoot Hawley Tariff Bill was to balance trade caused by importing cheap agricultural goods. In October 1929, the affirmation that the bill would become law caused the market to correct eight months before Herbert Hoover signed the bill. In September 1985, the United States and the G-7 devalued the dollar as a result of the Plaza Accord. This began currency distortions and interest rate hikes which eventually brought the markets down in October 1987. The international balance of payments is accounted for on a balance sheet and the attempt to rebalance this creates distortions, not solutions.

Many concerned citizens are unaware about their benefits from trade. During the famed "Battle for Seattle" in the late '90s, had the protesters stopped long enough to check the tags on the clothes they were wearing, they would be amazed to learn that they were protesting against a global economy in which they were willing and able participants; buying clothes from the entire world without realizing it. The factors that determine demand are: consumer preferences, resources and income, and price. Not where it is made. In essence, a shopper asks, "do I like it and can I afford it?"

If we want to raise the global standard of living we must open the trading lanes. There is growing protectionist fervor, especially in those developed nations who have benefited the most from open trading policies and now are acting to prevent the developing world from gaining from trade. If the wealthy nations want to be even wealthier, then allow businesses and other nations to earn higher profits by removing trading restrictions and allowing markets to flourish. Trade creates wealth. One of the most easily recognized and least researched evidence of this fact is demonstrated by markets and their reaction to our own trade policies.

As was true for the market's reaction to the Smoot Hawley Tariff, there is a direct relationship between the markets peaks and the trade. Conventional wisdom believes that the market lows in 2002 were caused by the "dot com bust." Specifics detail otherwise.

Evidence of this relationship is demonstrated graphically. Following the post September 11, 2001, low, the Dow Jones Industrial Average peaked on March 19, 2002, the day before the steel tariffs took effect. It did not cross its prior high until the steel tariffs were lifted. In 2004, the Europeans imposed tariffs and the markets did not recover until the Bush Administration announced its repeal of the Export Tax Credit, the cause of the European tariff. The reaction of the Dow Jones Industrial Average is illustrated.[12]

Figure 4.2

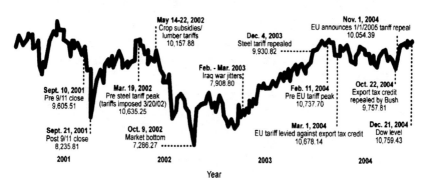

Free Trade and Stock Prices
Notable dates and the Dow Jones Industrial Average

Given this information, the immediate government actions should have been a repeal of these tariffs and not a cut in interest rates and a massive increase in the availability of easy credit, which led to the current economic crisis. When viewing charts such as these, it is important to understand what actually makes up the underlying value of stocks.

Stock prices are determined by many factors. The two most important are: will a company pay a dividend, either now or in the future and what are the future earnings of a company? In the past few years, there have been many theories about what elements make stocks go up or down: supply and demand, price to earnings ratios, dividend yields, etc. These, as well as others are very important, but earnings, specifically future earnings, are most critical. Decreased future earnings expectations reduce the present value of a security and also demand for the stock. When there are more sellers than buyers, stock prices fall.

The equity market is a leading economic indicator. Traditionally the market moves downward prior to an economic downturn and leads the economy out of a slowdown. Globally, capital markets moved rapidly and violently downward after September 14, 2008, predicting slower economic growth. The reaction of the governments of the world has been a fiscal and monetary stimulus, instead of free trade and currency stabilization. As we continue to erect protectionist barriers and destabilize the global means of exchange, currency, we risk further exacerbating the growing gap between the developed (wealthy) and non-developed (poor) world. One glaring example of this self destructive behavior regarding trade is crop subsidies.

Developed nations such as the United States, France and Germany overpay farmers to grow crops. Many other developed nations do, too. These nations have blocked the way for real farm subsidy reform in the current global trade round called the Doha Round. This policy, while lucrative for a few farmers in rich nations, results in an overproduction of crops. If the price is too high, a surplus occurs as corn and other grains rot on rail sidings due to fewer buyers wanting to purchase a good at an above market price.

Internationally, the opposite effect occurs. A surplus of crops in the developed world creates lower prices abroad, causing some third world farmers to pay more to plant than to harvest. International poverty is a result. Frustration, anger, misunderstanding and tyranny follows. Local and regional wars are often the final result of this policy failure.

Individual examples highlight the disparities. In Mali, cotton farmers struggle to make ends meet, tilling with scratch plows and oxen teams wondering if they will be able to make a profit at the harvest. In Mississippi, farmers in air conditioned tractors equipped with GPS and digital displays enjoy subsidies that insulate them from the despair of low prices in the third world.[13] In France, sugar farmers enjoy nearly triple the market price for their crop. In South Africa, farmers till acres of sugar cane by hand and walk miles to church. Many poor farmers lack basic necessities such as cars or tractors.[14]

For the world to prosper, forces of the free market must be allowed to function. Often markets are blamed for creating the world's problems, but in many cases, use of the free market has never been attempted.

It is vital to increase wealth in the poorest of regions. For a West African cotton farmer that exists on one dollar per day, increasing his income to three dollars a day is an enormous jump in his standard of living. Imagine the impact on an American if he or she made $70,000 per year and then immediately made $210,000 the next year. This increase of 300% for the poor farmer may be the difference of life and death for his malnourished children. It may be the difference between keeping rival gangs in the fields farming rather than being in the same fields planning an ambush. Linking countries like Zimbabwe, with its 1,700% annual inflation and 80% unemployment, to the rest of the world will help stabilize its current situation and create jobs.[15] The world is not ignorant of global poverty, but acts in a manner that often does not help.

For example, the relief of third world debt is a noble cause. This has been championed by many in Hollywood and in the music industry. They should be commended for their efforts. It would be easy for many of them, given the wealth they have earned, to ignore this as it has no direct effect on them. Celebrities' solutions to the debt relief problem are having lenders write off the loans. It will be far more difficult for the impoverished nations to get loans in the future if they do not pay them back. We should be helping them earn income to pay off these debts. The poorest nations of the world do not want our aid, they want our trade.

When nations receive aid, the competitiveness of exportable industries may be adversely affected. Aid can also make governments less responsive and less accountable to their citizens. In many cases, it is difficult to prove "any systematic relationship between aid and long term growth."[16] Corruption often is the result.

Often the arguments against trading with underdeveloped countries stem from prejudice against establishing relationships with those nations whose labor rates are lower than the developed world.

Job losses due to trade are a common argument, with lower wage jobs abroad, seen as the catalyst. Brink Lindsey's research shows that this anti-trade logic has existed for centuries.

> "The first and great disadvantage (of high wages) is that of being undersold by the French and Dutch in our principal manufactured goods," warned the English author of *Propositions for Improving the Manufactures, Agriculture and Commerce of Great Britain*, back in 1763. "The high price of labour is a fatal stab to the trade and manufactures of this country: and without the greatest care taken, it will in time be attended with very dreadful consequences."[17]

This mirrors the arguments of today regarding America's trade with China and Mexico. Trade may very well be the saving grace for the world, if we allow it.

Adam Smith comments:

> If a foreign country can supply us with a commodity cheaper than we ourselves can make it, better buy it of them with some part of the produce of our own industry, employed in a way in which we have some advantage.[18]

If there is to be a lessening of tensions globally, we must rapidly open the trading lanes. It will only be through an increase of the worldwide standard of living that the likelihood of global conflict will be diminished. Economic nationalism is increasing daily. The power of radicals to influence individuals is diminished if the individuals are empowered with liberty, choices and personal wealth. That wealth need not be only in monetary means.

As the world becomes more interconnected because of globalization, we ignore the wisdom of the ancients at our own peril: Plato and Aristotle on the benefits of trade, specialization and exchange; Smith on the invisible hand and free trade; Ricardo on comparative advantage of trade, Schumpeter on the concept of creative destruction, which is a result of specialization. In a global economy, economic considerations transcend political considerations. We need great economic policy today rooted in successful examples from the past.

There are not many factors, economic or otherwise, that can effect the economy all at once. Trade policy is one and currency stability is another. The British adopted free trade with the abolishment of the Corn Laws in 1846 and returned to the gold standard in 1821 following years of war with the United States and France. The United States developed its movement toward free trade in the twentieth century. In the nineteenth century, we demonstrated sound policy in adopting measures which fostered growth and deflation. There is no better combination than that of free trade with a stable currency, reinforced by the rule of law and private property rights. Trade is the cornerstone for global prosperity. It has a great side effect: peace. You don't wage war on your customers.

As trade forms the foundation for prosperity, currency facilitates the transactions. Currency stability remains the most neglected factor in domestic economic policy. Since the creation of the Federal Reserve in 1913, economic luminaries have often spoke of the need for a strong dollar and, yet implement policies which undermine the currency and create inflation. Chapter Five details the need for a strong currency and recommends congressional reforms for the Federal Reserve.

CHAPTER 5
TURN OFF THE PRINTING PRESS

*There is no such thing as a free lunch, especially
when you print the money.*

If the economy were compared to the human body, currency would be the bloodstream. Currency affects every cell in an economic system, be it an individual or business. It touches everyone all at once. The velocity of money, or the rate of exchange, is as important as ensuring that the veins and arteries in the human body are free from blockage.

Taken in its most basic role, currency is simply a means of exchange. It must be fungible and divisible. Currency should be a store of value and should be easily transferred between parties. People must easily recognize it. It must be accepted as payment for debts. In the case of gold or silver, this money provided through natural law, it is accepted in the marketplace without a decree or the words "legal tender." We instinctively know that gold and silver are worth something. Money avoids a double coincidence of wants. Simply stated, when you have currency and need something, you do not have to worry about finding a barter to trade for what you need.

Two important aspects of currency are stability and neutrality. In other words, it must be stable and it must favor no one. Currency stability allows for individuals and business to be able to project costs and depend on true profits, rather than inflation adjusted ones. If the currency is worth less every year, purchasing power is eroded and it takes more money to buy the same product. Rising prices do not necessarily equate to increased wealth.

A neutral currency favors no one. A policy of inflation favors those who have access to borrow money first, as they receive this money before prices rise and the currency is devalued.

The most important feature of a currency is the underlying trust that the value will not be rendered worth less over time. As the government violates the public trust over time allowing inflation, alternatives to the currency will be sought by global markets.

Inflation is one of the most detrimental domestic policies that the United States government carries out. Inflation is a monetary distortion caused by the government or central bank when it creates too much money, too quickly or in such a manner which the economy cannot absorb the infusion of credit or currency. Inflation benefits those who receive the money first before prices rise, hurts those on fixed income, devaluates the currency, encourages spending and discourages savings. Since the early 1900's, there is one common element at the end of all business cycles: permanently higher prices, especially in the capital goods sector.

Throughout history, there have been different types of inflation. In the sixteenth century, Spain experienced specie inflation as gold arrived from the new world and increased prices. In the nineteenth century United States, gold mining towns experienced this phenomenon, as miners brought more money into town. Whiskey may increase from one pinch of gold dust to two, depending on the merchant's ability to charge and the willingness of the miner to pay.

Debasement is a type of inflation that occurs when the monetary authorities substitute non-precious metal, such as lead for silver, as the United States did with its coins in 1965. The Romans did this to their coins toward the end of the empire.

Fiat inflation occurs when the government resorts to the physical printing of paper money. This type of inflation occurred in the United States during the Revolutionary War and the Civil War. France experienced this beginning in 1790 during the reign of terror. In the twentieth century, Germany resorted to the printing press in 1923 and 1924 with disastrous effects. Most recently, Zimbabwe has all but destroyed its currency by printing too much of it.

Repressed inflation occurs during the imposition of wage and price controls and the public is subjected to it once the controls are lifted. The United States experienced high inflation in 1946 after President Truman lifted wartime price controls.

The most common form of inflation in the modern age is fiduciary credit inflation and it is created electronically in the banking system by repeatedly loaning money. The United States has a fractional reserve banking system, which requires that only a fraction of the money loaned needs to be supported by money in the bank. This excess credit is loaned through the banking system with the "multiplier effect." Credit is loaned through the system and causes money creation to occur with a multiplier of 10.[1] Most money in circulation is not money in wallets or purses; it is in the form of demand deposits in banks commonly referred to as checkbook money.

The impact of fiduciary credit inflation is latent and occurs over time. It is subtle and the populace only realizes the slow creep of this inflation over a generation when, such as now, we pay for a car what our parent's paid for a house.

As this credit is expanded and loaned out year after year, the greatest danger to this system is a run on the banks, as most of the money is not in reserve. The weakness of credit expansion is now being felt by the entire global economy. In order to understand and fully appreciate this phenomenon, one must possess a basic understanding of the Federal Reserve and a brief overview of American monetary history.

The Federal Reserve is our central bank. Actually it is a system of twelve banks and twenty-five regional branches. The "Fed" as it is referred to, fulfills many roles. It regulates the banks and serves as the controller of the currency. The Fed is the government's bank and the bankers' bank. It regulates the money supply and secures much of the world's gold reserves. Most importantly, the Fed acts as a global clearing house for wires, checks and other transactions.[2] When it comes to maintaining the velocity of money, the Fed plays a vital role.

There were three promises made when the Federal Reserve was created in 1913. End all business cycles, end all bank failures and stabilize the value of the dollar. This system attempted to have a centralized body of decision makers adjust what markets had been able to do by themselves for years. This new system ignored the great economic progress, which occurred throughout the 1800's where wages doubled and doubled again and prices dropped.

The Federal Reserve implements monetary policy three ways: setting the discount rate, setting bank reserve requirements and conducting open market operations. The discount rate is the rate charged by the Federal Reserve to banks desiring overnight loans.[3] The Fed influences the target for the Fed funds rate. This is the rate at which member banks of the Federal Reserve System charge each other for overnight loans. This rate is targeted by the Fed and generally floats in a band.

Short term rates are set or influenced by the Federal Open Market Committee (FOMC). In eight regularly scheduled meetings per year, the FOMC meets to determine rates and assess the financial and economic state of the economy. The Committee consists of the Chairman and Vice Chairman of the Fed, the five Fed Governors and five Presidents of the Federal Reserve System, with one of those Presidents always being from the New York Fed.[4] Legend has it, that this was J.P. Morgan's influence. Morgan was a powerful New York banker who held much authority. All member's have equal vote, with the non-voting Presidents having a voice. The Presidents rotate in a voting status on an annual basis.

The second method of implementing monetary policy is setting reserve requirements in member banks. This is the most powerful and least often used tool of the Fed. If the Fed changes the reserve requirement it affects the entire banking system instantaneously. The rate is generally 10 percent, which means that the bank must keep $100 in reserve for every $1,000 deposited. This leads to inflation.

The final method of implementing monetary policy is open market operations. This occurs when the Fed purchases U.S. Treasury securities, bills, notes and bonds, in order to keep the government solvent. This is done through primary dealers. Open market operations allows the Fed to influence the target rate for overnight loans between banks. Open market operations ultimately results in the Fed cashing its own check and agreeing to hold government issues, whether through a primary dealer or going directly to the Treasury itself (known as monetizing the debt). The Federal Reserve did this on March 18, 2009, purchasing $300 billion in thirty year treasury bonds in an attempt to flatten the yield curve and lower long term interest rates, which are set by the market.

The history of the Fed can be traced back as early as the post revolutionary war days, when Alexander Hamilton, as George Washington's Treasury Secretary argued for a central bank for the fledging republic. There were two central banks prior to our current one. Both were disbanded, the second by Andrew Jackson. Both he and Thomas Jefferson despised the notion of one agency having charge of the money stock.

John Adams was of the opinion that bank bills that were issued beyond the amount of gold or silver in reserve represented a "cheat upon somebody."[5]

Without a central bank, the nation continued its westward expansion with economic panics. These "booms and busts" are common in business cycles. There were many major panics in this century: 1837, 1857, 1873 and 1893. The 1873 panic occurred when the United States was not on gold and was a result of corruption and speculation on the rapidly expanding railroads. The first major political scandal occurred during this time involving congress and a company called Credit Mobilier. It contributed to the depression and panic in the 1870's.

The nation left the gold standard to fund the Civil War and did not return to it until 1879. During the Civil War, the only instrument worth less than the greenback was confederate script. Once Treasury Secretary John Sherman placed the United States back on gold, the nation experienced 35 years of expansion, with deflation.

During the economic panic of 1907, J.P. Morgan had to import gold to the United States to keep American banks solvent, since people were demanding gold in exchange for their paper script. Morgan is credited with the belief that if you allow people access to their money, they will not want it. This event was the "last straw" in panics and gave rise to the desire to establish a central bank for the United States.

The following graph illustrates price stability afforded by a gold standard and the long term rise in prices when the standard is removed.[6]

Figure 5.1

Wholesale Price Index, United States
1800 - 1979

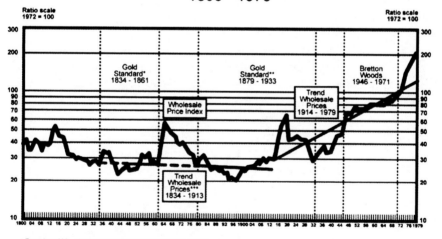

* Excludes 1838 - 1843 when specie payments were suspended
** United States imposes gold export embargo from September 1917 to June 1919
*** Broken line indicates years excluded in computing trend

During the period of 1880-1900 the total price decline was 10 percent and the gross domestic product more than doubled.[7] Between the late 1860's and the early 1890's savings and innovation increased, productivity soared and GNP increased at an average of 2 percent per year.[8] Modern economic theory ignores historical evidence that an economy can experience growth with deflation. Central bankers abhor the thought of falling prices and possess an inflationary bias in policymaking. Few individuals realize that the Fed's creation was based on the desire to offer stabilization to the economy and the currency. The effect has been the opposite of the intent.

Although most Americans believe that the Federal Reserve is an independent body, there is a direct relationship between the Fed and the Congress with collusion from the Treasury. The Fed is no more independent from the government than paint is from the wood is covers. The Fed encourages the government to spend more money than it receives when it acts as lender of last resort and buys treasuries. An example of lack of independence is illustrated by projections calculated in 2005 as to when the national debt would reach GDP.

The nominal GDP in 2005 was $12.487 trillion. The annual growth rate from 2001-2005 was 5.38 percent. The national debt at the end of fiscal year 2005 stood at $7.93 trillion. The growth of the debt during this period was 8.11 percent. In 2005, had current trends remained, the debt would have been equal to GDP in the year 2023 at $32 trillion.[9] This would alarm the world's creditors and place the dollar as one of the least desired currencies due to the devaluation that will ensue as the government shows no restraint at the printing press.

This calculation occurred several years before our current financial crisis. By July 2009, the United States the national debt totaled $11.4 trillion. GDP may continue to contract from roughly $14 trillion. The national debt may equal GDP in a few short years.

Global powers have viewed this development and have begun to make contingency plans. China has called for a super currency to replace the dollar. Russia may now begin accepting rubles for its oil in lieu of dollars. There is distant thunder in the currency markets and it should be cause for alarm in Washington. Inaction by government officials regarding this developing crisis is most concerning.

Figure 5.2

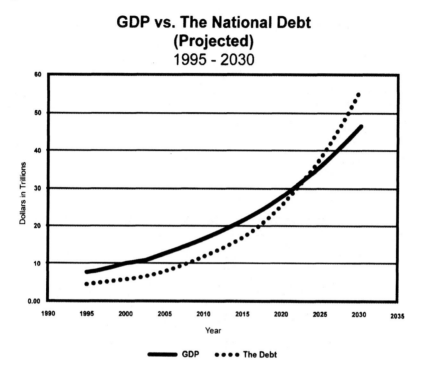

GDP vs. The National Debt
(Projected)
1995 - 2030

Since the early 1980's, the total debt has increased from $1 trillion to $11.4 trillion and interest rates have decreased. This does not mean that there are no consequences to our ballooning debt. For every action, there is an equal and opposite reaction. Newton's Third Law of physics is applicable to economics and finance. There are no solitary events in an economy, especially in a global economy.

Increased supply of both dollars and debt and not enough demand, equates to falling currency prices. The old way of viewing the impact of the debt was called the "crowding out effect." This theory advocated the belief that government borrowing would cause interest rates to rise by removing capital from the banking system and crowding out business and individuals. As rates dropped to very low levels in the first half of this new decade, politicians and economists viewed increased levels of debt with no alarm at all. In fact, rising levels of debt have been dismissed out right.

This explains Vice President Cheney's famous statement that, "Ronald Reagan proved that deficits don't matter." They do, but observers must now look away from the traditional measure of distortion, which implied a fixed amount of money available. Now, there is an increased amount created by the Federal Reserve conducting open market operations in order to keep the government solvent. Further, total interagency debt totals over $4 trillion, which the market views as inflationary. Most economists focus only on "public debt," but any rational person cannot ignore the total debt.

In the past few years, gold has also signaled inflation. Dismissed as archaic and only an indicator of world event risk, gold is too old of a currency to be ignored. As of this writing, gold is nearing $1,000 per ounce.

Table 5.1

Dollar Weakness Correlated to the National Debt

Date	National Debt (trillions)	Gold (per oz.)	Oil (per bbl.)	Euro	Fed Funds
09/30/08	$10.024	$870.00	$100.70	$1.4081	2.00%
09/30/07	9.007	743.10	82.86	1.4219	4.75
09/30/06	8.506	598.70	62.90	1.2687	5.25
09/30/05	7.932	468.70	66.21	1.2058	3.75
09/30/04	7.379	418.40	49.56	1.2417	1.75
09/30/03	6.783	384.70	29.19	1.1650	1.00
09/30/02	6.228	323.80	30.59	0.9879	1.75
09/30/01	5.807	291.55	23.44	0.9099	3.00
09/30/00	5.674	273.80	30.87	0.8837	6.50

Sources
National Debt: Department of the Treasury[10]
Gold: Kitco Bullion Dealers[11]
Oil: U.S. Energy Information Administration[12]
Exchange Rates: x-rates.com[13]
Fed Funds Rate: NY Federal Reserve[14]

The world has not witnessed such an increase in gold since the 1970's when the policies of Lyndon Johnson and Richard Nixon caused massive inflation and gold reached $800 per ounce. Funding the war on poverty and Vietnam, as well as Nixon failing to hold the gold exchange standard caused the inflationary price spike. Combined with the oil shocks and a poorly run Fed under G. William Miller, the nation lost control of its currency for nearly a decade. We run that risk again.

Oil continued to increase as the commodity is priced in dollars and when foreigners spend dollars, they possess less purchasing power. Oil producers demand more dollars for the same product to compensate for the devaluation. To make matters worse, inflation over the years has been recently exacerbated by unrestrained spending by the Bush Administration. The Administration's intent was to stimulate the economy in the same manner Ronald Reagan did, by a supply side stimulus. Tax revenues may have increased, but the national debt doubled.

Two graphs illustrate the reaction of gold to domestic events. This demonstrates how gold reacted to the re-election of President Bush and the nomination of Dr. Ben Bernanke to be chairman of the Federal Reserve. The third big movement in the gold market occurred after Congress increased the debt ceiling from $8.3 trillion to $8.9 trillion.[15]

Unfortunately, the problem is that the government did not cut spending; the deficit increased as has the national debt. You can't run the economy on a credit card. Warren Buffett warned, "Borrowed money is the most common way smart guys go broke."[16] The same principle applies to government.

Figure 5.3

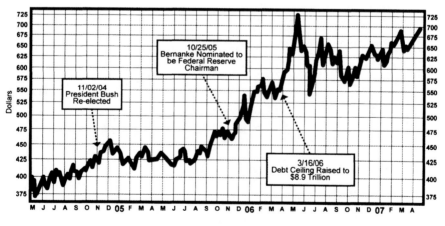

Gold Reacts to Domestic Events
2004 - 2006

Gold Dollars Per Ounce

The second graph shows a continuation of the upward trend in gold due to the expansion of the national debt.[17]

Observing Federal Reserve actions in 2007, as the Fed begins decreasing the Fed funds rate and Congress raises the debt ceiling again, the price of gold escalates.

Figure 5.4

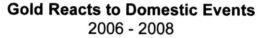

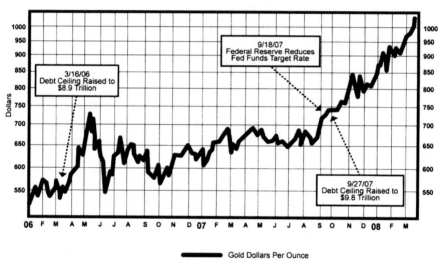

Gold Reacts to Domestic Events
2006 - 2008

Gold Dollars Per Ounce

Milton Friedman provides his own warning.

> Fiduciary money is a contract to pay standard money. It so happens that there is a long interval between the making of such a contract and its realization. This enhances the difficulty of enforcing the contract and hence also the temptation to issue fraudulent contracts. In addition, once fiduciary elements have been introduced, the temptation for government itself to issue fiduciary money is almost irresistible.[18]

Friedman added an interesting thought about the end result of this process: "Inflation is taxation without legislation."[19]

Adam Smith also commented on government's debauchery:

For in every country of the world, I believe, the avarice and injustice of princes and sovereign states, abusing the confidence of their subjects, have by degrees diminished the real quality of metal, which had been originally contained in their coins. The Roman As, in the latter stages of the Republick, (sic.) was reduced to the twenty-forth part of its original value...[20]

Hans Sennholz stated, "We must reject the basic psychological maxim that government can fool all of the people all of the time with easy money and credit."[21]

A practical result of this fiduciary credit inflation has been to drive the good money underground to safes, safe deposit boxes and homes. The market reaction is best characterized by Gresham's Law which states, "Bad money drives out good money." When the governments throughout history debase or inflate their currency the result is the same.

The creation of excess credit as a method of economic stimulus has weakened the dollar, as the world views this expansion as fiscally irresponsible. A low dollar raises the price of imports. Domestic goods that compete with imports cost more, too. American manufacturers can raise prices without loss of market share.

Ordinarily, trade and global competition keep prices lower, but fiduciary credit inflation has negated this positive check in the world economic system. Temporary or permanent tariffs and quotas on many items such as steel and lumber combined with the inflationary forces of a massive federal debt to keep prices moving higher.

Another danger of pursuing policies that weaken the dollar is that America punishes its foreign lenders for financing our debt, rather than rewarding them. Foreigners have always been willing to invest in treasuries since they have been viewed as risk free. The declining dollar now brings added currency risk into the equation. Foreigners hold $2 trillion of government paper. How long does the government expect a rational investor to receive $8 billion interest while losing $10 billion in principal on a currency swap?

With the government adding to the national debt at the rate of $3.5 billion per day, it is a good bet that the dollar will not strengthen in a meaningful fashion. To embrace the notion that the nation can continue to simply create money and not have it impact anything else is a belief so steeped in ignorance it almost defies description. Japan, China, Russia and other nations have begun to diversify their foreign reserves, i.e. dump the dollar. American companies who deal with foreign suppliers often receive requests that estimates for jobs be made in Euros, not dollars. This is the real market at work.

In a global economy, capital will have to go where it will grow. Should the dollar continue to decline, foreigners will look for alternate investments that carry equal or less risk and will render a positive rather than a negative return.

Many foreigners have not forgotten when Nixon closed the gold window in August 1971, leaving them with diluted paper as America fought the war on poverty and the war in Vietnam, relying on the printing press. Although this action occurred one generation ago, investors always remember when you break a contract. They will act in their own self interest to ensure it does not happen again.

In March 2009, Chinese Premier Wen Jiahao expressed concern over the growing U.S. debt and the security of these instruments. "Frankly speaking, I do have some worries."[22] Lawrence Summers, President Obama's chief economic advisor offered a highly Keynesian response in defense of deficit spending, "If you don't prime the pump and you allow the process of decay and decline and deleveraging to continue, it's much more costly to do it later."[23] This statement does little to calm foreign investors and makes it more likely that the dollar will weaken near term. Having been "burned" once by the United States, foreigners could still make a market based decision and abandon further treasury purchases. Congressman John Tanner most accurately summarized our reliance on foreign lending, "If China attacked Taiwan, we would have to borrow money from China to defend Taiwan."[24] There is a domestic precedent that illustrates the market rejecting the government's debt obligations.

In 1992, California faced a budget crisis. By the end of June, the legislators and Governor Pete Wilson were unable to resolve an $11 billion shortfall in revenues. The state began issuing registered warrants in lieu of checks to cover payments. Banks and financial institutions processed the checks, until the state's ability to meet its obligations began to be questioned. On July 24th, Bank of America said it would stop accepting the warrants on August 5th. Later, Wells Fargo began rejecting warrants. Other banks followed.[25] Global markets could do the same to our treasury paper at any time.

The Federal Reserve's stated goal of "price stability" when viewed in periods of decades, rather than quarters, has been a complete and total failure. Infusions of excess fiduciary credit into the banking system only result in permanently higher prices in the capital goods sector of the economy. In short, a ratchet effect in which prices move in one direction:

up. This price inflation exacerbates the divide between the haves and have-nots, as inflation favors those with real assets and market power. This is an issue that liberals and conservatives agree, but cannot identify the root cause or solution.

An inflationary policy by the central bank, the simple creation of money without backing, represents an assault on individual liberty and private property rights. As the currency is devalued decade after decade, it takes more money to buy the same items. Further,

> Governments are eager to apply coercion to mitigate the unpopular effects of their own inflation. With growing popular support they resort to such comprehensive measures as price, wage and rent controls. They substitute public expenditure for shrinking private investment. They formulate "development plans" and create new bureaucracies for implementation.[26]

A government program that is a direct result of inflation is the minimum wage. It is a job destroyer. This policy treats a symptom, not the cause. The cause is a devaluating currency. As government expands the money supply faster than the economy grows, inflation occurs. A minimum wage mandates what business must pay rather than have business calculate what a job is worth based on four factors: cost of inputs, technology, price of goods sold and profits. A minimum wage is a price floor which creates an excess of labor at a given price and a lack of demand for that labor by employers. A surplus of labor ensues. When government mandates a cost on business involving pay increases, it often neglects other costs business must bear, such as increased payroll taxes.

In 1998, Harriet Cane owner of the Sweet Life Restaurant in Marietta, Georgia, wrote an editorial in *The Wall Street Journal* warning the Clinton Administration not to raise the minimum wage. She employed mostly teenagers and working mothers. At the time of the writing she employed nine; she had previously employed 16. If passed, the Clinton Administration's proposal would have directly increased her monthly payroll by $570. This did not include the increase in employer paid payroll taxes, unemployment insurance and workman's compensation.[27] The outcome of her situation is unknown.

Inflation impacts all of us and needs to be brought under control. One method of controlling inflation would be to use the price of gold as an indicator. As the United States gold reserves are low, the dollar could not be made redeemable by the treasury for gold. The traditional gold standard may not work. This may be too cumbersome in the age when $2 trillion move through international markets daily. Any mention of policy considerations and gold would certainly be met with consternation and, in some quarters, laughter. The government and academia may believe themselves immune to the warnings of a 5,000 year old currency, but should understand the following:

> Gold is the barometer of public confidence in fiat money, and it is difficult to rebuild confidence in a currency once it has been allowed to slide. Gold has been a reliable harbinger of many economic troubles-not just of escalating prices at the gas pumps, but of inflation, rising interest rates, stagnation and poor investment performance on the part of bonds and equities alike. Changes on the price of gold are excellent predictors of all of these. The dollar's collapse is nothing less than a body blow to capitalism.[28]

There is a very good reason that the Constitution specifies that the payments of debts be paid in gold and silver.[29] Having lived through the Revolution, the framers understood the value of sound money. The phrase, "it ain't worth a Continental," derived from the worthlessness of the Continental Dollar printed in such amount, that it was devalued throughout the war, resulting in inflation. The enlightened men of the time may have also been aware of the debauchery of the Roman currency by Nero and Diocletian, whose coin clipping and later debasement, ruined the empire's means of exchange.

Ludwig von Mises warns about the terrible consequences of inflation:

> It leads everyone to consume his fortune; it discourages saving, and thereby prevents the formation of fresh capital. It encourages the confiscatory policy of taxation.[30]

If the United States used the price of gold as a signal to adjust monetary policy, the nation would experience huge capital inflows due to the long standing desire of investors to seek currency stability in whatever form were offered. Long term interest rates would drop immediately as the market would eliminate some of the inflation premium present in the current rate of interest. This component in interest rates is equal to the rate of expectation demanded by the lender that the borrower may default. This return to a use of the price of gold by the United States would be viewed globally as a desire of the nation to stop the ninety six years of inflationary policies pursued by central bankers, schooled in Keynesian economic theory.

Gold is a historic and accurate gauge of inflation. As a general benchmark we could target gold at the marginal cost of production, increasing interest rates as gold rose above this price and decreasing rates as gold dropped below it. A target price could also be determined by viewing a 200 day moving average of gold. Other common sense methods could be used. The bottom line: gold can no longer be ignored when determining monetary policy and its signals to the market must be recognized.

Politicians and economists often blame currency weakness on the trade deficit. The dollar is not low because of a trade deficit; it's low because there is a global excess of dollars, represented by electronic and physical currency, as well as too many U.S. Treasury debt instruments. Raising interest rates will not strengthen the dollar near term. Only fiscal responsibility, by the White House and Congress, will increase the value of the currency. The Obama Administration is benefiting by a dollar that is retaining its value on international exchanges, as the central banks of the world are engaged in quantitative easing, weakening their currencies and engaging in their own stimulus. It is as some experts are saying, "a race to the bottom."

If the price of gold were to be ignored in monetary policymaking, another solution would be to have Congress remove the Federal Reserve's authority from setting short term interest rates. These rates could be affected by supply and demand, just like long term rates are. Further, congress could prohibit government agencies, including the Federal Reserve from buying Treasury issues. The ability of the Fed to create money faster than the economy can grow has fostered an environment in which the cost of a car for our generation is equivalent to the price paid for a house for our parent's generation. Congress should revoke parts of the Federal Reserve Act of 1913.

The Executive Branch could strengthen the currency by submitting a balanced budget to Congress. The President should use his authority to sell assets to raise capital to pay down existing debt. The government places too much importance on the Federal Reserve's balance sheet, which is a result of electronically created assets and not enough time focusing on the national balance sheet. The United States owns land, buildings, coastline and many other assets. The government must sell these assets to eliminate deficits. Deficits are a natural outgrowth of unrestrained politics and the national debt causes inflation and devalues the

currency. Many of our global business partners and lenders are express-
ing grave concerns about the integrity of the dollar and should these
warnings go unheeded, we may experience a currency crisis of unprecedented proportion.

Paul Johnson, the eminent British author and historian, rendered sage
advice to Prime Minister Margaret Thatcher on the roles of government.
"There are three things the government must handle, for no one else can:
external defense, internal order and maintaining an honest currency."[31]
He added as governments tend to do more the three "musts" begin to be
neglected. The most likely of these three to be overlooked is the currency. Johnson warns, "Do-everything governments nearly always allow
inflation to gain a hold." [32]

CHAPTER 6
YOU CAN'T BLAME THE MONARCH

The government is not the source of wealth.

The prior two chapters outlined guidelines and presented a philosophy to formulate sound trade and currency policies. This chapter provides ideas for tax reform. The intent is to redirect the course of national tax policy in order to increase our standard of living and increase tax revenue. Once this is achieved, global reforms can be more easily accomplished. As we set an example for other nations, they will be more willing to take steps to ensure greater stability and prosperity, once they understand it is in their own self interest to do so.

In many cases, government at all levels has made itself the gatekeeper or approving authority of business deals, relationships and contracts. With its ability to make laws in exchange for political contributions, the government rules with a "wink and a nod." This has probably been the case since the beginning of time. This may not change completely, but it is important to be aware of the enormous cost of the current system.

The national income tax code is a very damaging system that should be reformed. The code is a result of years of lobbying. The current system results in billions of hours wasted in preparing, avoiding and consulting others about federal taxes. Taxes reduce economic activity and diminish incentives. A new system needs to be developed. A graduated flat tax is the most easily understood and fairest system. By being graduated, this will eliminate most of the complaints about the nature of this type of tax system.

In addition to the economic benefit, the greatest improvement due to the adoption of a national flat tax is that it would eliminate most of the lobbying and unfair tax treatment that is created through campaign contributions. If there were no opportunity to create loopholes, there would be less lobbying. The format would need to have breakpoints to address the issue of the regressive nature of the tax. The tax should be at eighteen percent. There would be no tax for those who made less than $20,000. Individuals making between $20,000 and $40,000 would pay six percent, those earning between $40,000 and $60,000 would pay twelve percent. The eighteen percent would be borne by those earning over $60,000. Budget shortfalls resulting from an adoption from this tax would be addressed through budget cuts and department closings at all levels of government.

The Obama Administration has made it very clear that it intends to allow the Bush tax cuts of 2001 to expire and have the rich pay their fair share. Numerous studies over the past decade prove that the top ten percent of income earners already pay a majority of the taxes. The administration also believes that it can pay for half of national health care by a tax increase. This is linear logic in a non-linear universe. Tax revenues will decrease as top income earners buy municipal bonds, invest in real estate or avoid the tax in some legal manner.

What is most interesting in this confiscatory philosophy is that lawmakers fail to realize that most individuals who make over $250,000 per year hire everyone that makes less than $250,000 per year. It is completely unrealistic to believe that business owners will absorb a tax increase and reduce their standard of living. The greatest expenses that a business incurs are payroll and taxes. As business cannot reduce its own taxes, it will reduce its payroll. Higher taxes lead to higher unemployment.

The State of Michigan is an example. In 2007, lawmakers desired to eliminate the Single Business Tax which taxed gross revenue, not net income. In essence, a business could lose money and still owe taxes. When a compromise could not be reached, the state introduced the Michigan Business Tax which raised taxes on some businesses 500 percent. The state also increased the state income tax. Combined with a loss of automotive jobs and a unionized workforce, the state has the highest unemployment rate in the nation, over fourteen percent. Business does not lose money willingly. Owners will maintain their going concern until they are the only employee remaining. Many firms began as operations with less than five people. The entrepreneur never forgets how to stay in business with minimal overhead. Owners will not lose their homes as a result of a tax increase; employees will lose their jobs.

One of the best examples of how taxes influence behavior can be found in the Luxury Tax of 1990. With President George H. W. Bush going back on his "no new taxes pledge," lawmakers believed that the rich would not allow an additional ten percent tax alter their spending habits on "toys." How wrong they were.

The tax almost destroyed the American yachting industry. One company, Viking Yachts, went from a payroll of 1,500 in two plants to 80 employees in one plant. Bob Healey, Viking's owner, borrowed working capital to keep the company solvent and organized a national protest in Washington.[1] The luxury taxes took in $97 million less in the first year than had been projected. Hardest hit were the blue collar workers, whose livelihood depended on the purchasing power of the wealthy to buy their products. In the first year alone, yacht sales dropped seventy seven percent and 25,000 employees lost their jobs. In 1996, Congress repealed the tax on most luxury goods, but it took until 2003 to totally phase out the tax on luxury cars.[2] Judging by the promised repeal of the 2001 tax cuts, we have learned nothing.

Rather than modify behavior in a negative manner, the government should move in a positive direction. The chart below illustrates the net increase in tax revenue during the 1980's. The deficit increased because of runaway spending, not a decrease in revenue.[3]

Table 6.1

Impact of Reagan Era Tax Cuts on Revenue
1981-1988
(in billions)

Year	Receipts	Outlays	Deficit
1981	$599	$678	$79
1982	618	746	128
1983	601	808	208
1984	666	851	185
1985	734	946	212
1986	769	990	212
1987	854	1,004	149
1988	909	1,064	155

Differences due to rounding.

A few examples of the cumulative effects of taxation are shown below. This is not a complete list. When you add all the taxes we pay, we work more than six months to finally begin working for ourselves. When most in the media talk of tax freedom day, they only look at the first column. No one discusses the third column, as many do not understand that business ultimately does not pay tax; consumers pay all taxes.

Table 6.2

Selected Examples of Taxation

Income	Other	Business
Federal	State Sales	FICA
State	Gasoline	FUTA
FICA	ATF	SUTA
AMT	Cable	Federal
City	Capital Gains	State
Interest Income	Dividends	Personal Property
	Estate	Licensure
	Licensure	Airport Fees
	Phone	Transportation/Highway
	Property	Workman's Compensation
	Toll Roads	

The total tax against annual income would be roughly thirty percent, ten percent, and fifteen percent respectively. This must change.

Proponents of tax cuts for the middle class and higher taxes for the rich ignore the fact that if you take capital away from business owners, fewer jobs will be created. FDR tried this with the Revenue Act of 1934, reducing taxes for those earning between $5,000 and $9,000, while raising taxes on those making over $9,000.[4] Attempting to redistribute wealth ignores the fact that wealth or income is not distributed at all. Wealth is earned, created, saved and spent.[5]

The government's desire to redistribute wealth ignores the spirit of the human condition. Roughly eighty percent of the wealth in the United States is controlled by twenty percent of the people. If the government were to evenly distribute this wealth, in five years, eighty percent of the wealth would be controlled by twenty percent of the people. Entrepreneurs know how to create wealth and they understand what it takes to keep it. Larry Reed, President Emeritus of the Mackinac Center stated, "Where people are free, they are not equal and where people are equal, they are not free."[6] From an economic standpoint, there will always be differences in the standard of living, as individuals apply themselves in various endeavors with different levels of aptitude throughout their lives. The role of government is to encourage individual initiative, not vilify people for it.

Capital gains taxes are favorite targets of politicians to punish the rich for the accumulation of "excess wealth." The irony is that the higher the capital gains tax, the lower the revenue. Ultimately, a capital gains tax is not a tax on capital; it is a tax on the formation of capital. When the government increases capital gains taxes, money which would be formed to produce capital generally moves to three areas: municipal securities, real estate or offshore accounts. All options limit tax exposure. It is not evasion; it is avoidance. Reduced rates on capital gains produce greater tax revenue.[7]

Figure 6.1

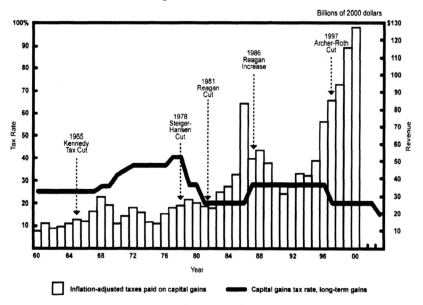

Top Capital Gains Tax Rate and Inflation-Adjusted Federal Revenue

Source: U.S. Department of the Treasury, Office of Tax Analysis

The payroll tax is another tax that is in need of reform. Social security should be modified. The first option would be to allow people to remain involved in the system as is. Their employer and employee Federal Insurance Contribution Act (FICA) taxes would go into the general fund. The second option would allow individuals to be bought out, similar to a severance package, with this money being rolled into an IRA with the same mandatory requirements as IRA's regarding withdrawals, with the exception that an individual would be unable to cash out all at once. All future employee FICA contributions would be invested into the employees IRA. The employer FICA would go into the general fund. This would ensure that the system for those remaining would not be bank-rupted by a massive defection of those of us who would leave the system en masse.

An example of how to modify the payroll tax and handle the "eas-ing" of some of the population off social security is outlined below. As each succeeding group ages, they can be allowed to pay less into the sys-tem.

This method will allow the system not to suffer a catastrophic loss of revenue as the baby boomers retire, but as they begin to pass away, less will be required as an input, freeing most workers to stop putting into the system, as long as they elect to opt out of the system. If means testing is adopted, this would work especially well. Individuals would be able to self direct their savings into their own accounts. The current withholding rate is 6.2 percent for employees and corporations.

Table 6.3

Recommended Payroll Tax Rollback

Age	2015	2020	2030	2040	2050
16-20	0.2%	0.0%	0.0%	0.0%	0.0%
21-30	1.2%	0.2%	0.0%	0.0%	0.0%
31-40	2.2%	1.2%	0.2%	0.0%	0.0%
41-50	3.2%	2.2%	1.2%	0.2%	0.0%
50+	4.2%	3.2%	2.2%	1.2%	0.2%

If no long term market based reform is adopted, the government will most likely adopt the following measures. First, it will raise the cap on current limits past $106,800 to several hundred thousand. This will in-crease revenues, but not enough. Second, the government will increase employer FICA withholding, thus punishing businesses, but hiding the tax to employees. That is, until workers are not able to get a raise the fol-lowing year; then they will understand. Finally, the government will in-crease the age that individuals may collect social security.

Common sense needs to rule. The Social Security system needs to provide for retirement only. All of the programs that have developed over the decades that are related to this program have bankrupted the system. Social security should be means tested, meaning that individuals having an income level over a certain amount or a given level of savings over a specified amount will no longer be eligible to receive benefits. This decision would violate a social contract made in 1935, but the government has extended itself beyond reasonable repair and measures must be implemented to arrest the runaway growth of this entitlement plan.

Mark Skousen, an Austrian Economist and author, said in March 2001, that if we means tested social security, he believed that the tax could drop from 6.2 percent to 4.2 percent.[8] The intent of this New Deal program began by FDR was to assist individuals who would be eligible at a certain age to draw this money until they died in a few years. This program now includes Supplemental Social Security Income. Another related program allows older parents to draw money for their children, even if they have means. This system is bankrupting itself. It must be fixed without delay.

Addressing the taxation of savings is another priority. Savings is the key element of capitalism. Combining the positive effects of savings with the long term returns of the market provides a sound argument for modifying the current social security system. This policy also reinforces private property rights, as individuals are afforded the opportunity to take ownership of their own assets. Tax rates on savings accounts should be minimal to encourage capital formation. Given the current economic crisis, it is far more desirable for individuals and business to recapitalize the banks than have the government credit the banks with electronic money that will only lead to inflation in the future.

Consumption taxes are another method that the government lurches for when more revenue is needed. Gambling is the worst form of consumption tax. States and municipalities that turn to gambling as a solution reduced tax revenue, poison the very human capital that they are dependent on to solve their problems. States begin selling the idea of gambling, by telling the residents that profits from the new lottery will go to the schools. This later leads to municipal sponsored gambling with casinos, sold to the public as a job creator. Then other cities approach the state with the geographical argument, "If this city has a casino, why can't we?"   While this is occurring, the lottery begins to appear on nightly TV. Worse, lottery drawings are held twice a day.

Further, Keno is introduced, giving the populace the ability to lose money on an hourly basis. Gambling is now allowed online or in establishments that serve alcohol. Credit card use is allowed. This policy rests on social and moral quicksand. It is an example of government at its very, very worst and is a mockery of Ronald Reagan's biblical reference to a shining city on a hill.

President Washington called gambling, "The child of avarice, the brother of iniquity, the father of mischief."[9] Gambling reinforces the worst lesson in human behavior; the belief that you can get something for nothing. The social ills are long and well documented. Gambling contributes to addiction; it results in personal bankruptcies; it reinforces undesirable behavior; it reallocates resources to unproductive uses; it destroys families and lives. It encourages spending and reduces savings. This list is virtually endless. If business provides gaming facilities as a recreational choice that is a different issue. When government sponsors gambling, it risks permanently damaging the citizens for which government represents.

The modern tax code requires immediate reform. In all areas: income, savings, capital gains, payroll and consumption, we must improve our method of collecting revenue to keep the necessary functions of government funded while providing incentives to job creators and workers. Increased business activity results in higher net income and elevated tax revenue. History supports this assertion.

CHAPTER 7
BRAIN DEAD AND CHARGING AHEAD

You cannot blame capitalism for the failures of socialism.

This brief chapter can be summed up in two words: unenlightened bene-volence. It is the genuine desire to do good without having the faintest idea of the second order consequences that the action will produce. Usually, the effect is the opposite of the intent. Ronald Reagan warned us to be very cautious if we ever heard this phrase: "I am from the govern-ment and I am here to help you." The issue here is more of a social na-ture and highlights the underlying theme of economics: how people re-spond to incentives. As in the previous chapters, the intent is to adopt locally and reform globally. This chapter does not "flow" in a traditional sense, but there are two general threads of continuity. First, is human capital development. The second is cost savings to the nation. Three areas will be discussed: healthcare, prison reform and poverty. In order to allow the have-nots to become haves, reforming these areas would help.

The rising cost of healthcare could very well be our undoing. With an increasingly gray population and skyrocketing costs, the federal budg-et is under great duress. During the 1990's healthcare fight, the most of-ten quoted statistic regarding the size of healthcare expenditures was one seventh of GDP. It is now reaching one fifth of GDP.

The solution must be more market based, not more government based. Years ago, Milton Friedman gave an interview on television.[1] Friedman made an analogy between the healthcare cost problem and car insurance covering an oil change. If your auto insurance covered your oil changes, how much would the oil change cost? A lot more, since your insurance company, rather than you, paid the bill. The core issue here is known as third party payer.

Many desire to change our current system. However, the politicians, who are trying to bring you a form of the Canadian health care system, never lived in Canada. It is interesting to hear Senator Kennedy from Massachusetts speak about the need to reform our health care system, with the understanding that he did not leave the United States to have brain surgery.

Examples of flaws in the Canadian system are many. When my wife's grandmother suffered a stroke in Windsor, Ontario, she was not afforded an MRI or CAT Scan. Although she was eighty at the time, there was only one MRI machine in the entire city. She did not qualify under the rationed system for a screening. She was sent home.

A graduate student of mine relayed a story about her father-in-law, also a resident of Windsor. He needed bypass surgery and needed to travel to London, Ontario to receive treatment. However, after examination, he was deemed too old for the surgery and was sent home. It was only through extraordinary efforts from his son, who had been a doctor in Canada for four years, did he finally receive treatment.

On August 16, 2007, Karen Jepp gave birth to identical quadruplets. The children were born in the city of Great Falls, Montana. Following the births and care, the family returned home to Calgary, Alberta. They were Canadian citizens. As the mother went into labor, the hospital in Calgary could not provide adequate care in the neo-natal unit for four premature newborns. Doctors and staff telephoned other hospitals in the country without success. Finally, Benefis Healthcare Hospital, 300 miles to the south, agreed to accept the mother and an emergency flight ensued. The American system worked.[2]

There are many other examples. The bottom line: when our Canadian neighbors need immediate and great care, they cross the border and write checks. Don't let anyone on the campaign trail try and tell you otherwise. Comparing Canada, population of thirty one million, to the United States, population of over 300 million and assuming equal problems and solutions demonstrates only ignorance.

In 2006, Massachusetts adopted a "universal" health care system. Costs are now skyrocketing. The state's overall costs on healthcare have increased 42 percent since 2006. Price controls may follow. A panel appointed by Governor Deval Patrick is considering limiting coverage, excluding services and other measures. The state has already raised premiums, taxed insurers and increased business penalties.[3]

Current options being considered to pay for this new plan is a tax against income for those earning over $250,000 per year. A second option is taxation of all of those individuals who do not join the government plan. This action would punish individuals for exercising free choice in selecting a service provider. Should government levy additional taxes against business in a time of severe recession, business owners will have no choice but to curtail health benefits to millions of Americans.

Although forty six million Americans are uninsured, having the government fix the problem it has created will only complicate matters and increase an already distorted system. Consumers have to bear more of the cost. A provider cannot charge what the consumer cannot pay. Health savings accounts must be expanded and government must facilitate the environment for the solution rather than mandate one. In short, a government plan is no plan. Further, government cannot solve a market problem. This problem demands market reform based on supply and demand, quality of care and a solution to third party payer. Decreasing the number of poor in the United States would certainly ease the burden on our heath care system.

Domestic poverty is the result of the failure of domestic policy. Since 1965, the United States has spent roughly $4 trillion to eliminate poverty. Many current programs cause benefits to be lost all at once. In the inner cities, we have effectively replaced 300 years of physical slavery with 150 years of economic slavery.

While there are many examples of success stories of Americans whose ancestors grew up in the city or were decedents of slaves, the vast majority of African-Americans remain trapped in the most violent and economically distraught sections of our largest urban areas. The American dream remains just that. The phrase, "Our prosperity is dependent on the prosperity of our neighbor," does not just apply to our trading partners, it applies to our cities, counties and states. To believe that wealthy America can "hide" in the suburbs and effectively ignore the inner cities is to believe that your taxes are only spent in your local municipality. If there is trouble somewhere in your state, you will pay for it.

The real issue is not: why are individuals poor? That is a simple question. They don't have money or tangible assets. The real issue is: why aren't they wealthy? Many of the poor aren't wealthy because they are trapped in a system that if they make over a certain amount of money, they would lose all of their benefits at once. For example, in order to qualify for Supplemental Social Security Income (SSI), individuals are allowed certain assets including: a house and land, car, burial plot, a small amount of cash and a minimal cash value in a life insurance policy. Some income is not included when determining eligibility.[4] But if an individual were to amass too many resources, over $2,000 for individuals or $3,000 for couples, they would be in danger of losing their SSI. Income caps work the same way. If individuals were to earn more than their allowable amount and lose benefits that were equal to even $1.00 more than that amount, it would make no sense to work, unless the benefit gained were greater than the alternative forgone.

When we moved back to the Detroit area in 1992, I remember leaving a local grocery store. Outside stood a man with a sign, "Will work for food." I stopped and told him that there was a help wanted sign at a Wendy's about a block away. He told me he could not work or he would lose all of his benefits. In all of the textbooks I have reviewed at the graduate and undergraduate levels, I have never read one that addressed this issue.

This issue is illustrated graphically below. The horizontal axis depicts the income earned, the vertical axis benefits received. In the first illustration, the individual has his benefits taken away all at once when a certain income or savings level is achieved. In the second illustration, a gradual reduction of benefits is allowed.

Figure 7.1

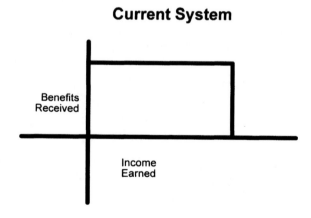

Current System

Figure 7.2

Recommended System

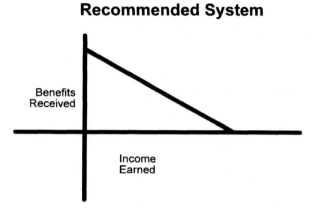

Benefits
Received

Income
Earned

For those federal and state programs that already have a graduated scale, taxation contributes to trapping individuals in poverty. A brilliant and wide ranging study by the Center for Public Finance Research of the State of Minnesota demonstrates the following:

> Lower income households can face very high marginal tax. Rates from 60% to over 100% are common for households using a standard "package" of assistance programs that include health care, child care, available tax code provisions, and welfare cash and food assistance benefits.[5]

> A one parent/two child household using welfare and food assistance benefits, all generally available tax provisions, and direct subsidies for health insurance and child care faces marginal tax rates ranging from 50% to 250% between incomes of $23,500 and $41,700. Between $33,000 and $34,000, this household loses nearly $2.50 in benefits for the additional dollar of earned income.[6]

A rational person will not work in this situation. Why would an individual willingly lose money and/or benefits? This is a wide spread national problem that must be addressed immediately.

As with social security reform, the United States should not remove its citizens from social assistance programs at once. These programs have been enacted over decades; they must be reconfigured over time with much warning and education from the agencies that provide the funds. There needs to be great work done locally to foster improvement. Our elected lawmakers in Washington are too far removed from our cities and towns to accurately gage the correct method for modifying the programs that reinforce undesirable behavior. The best the federal government can do is create the proper atmosphere for decisions to be made. This is a tenth amendment issue that needs local input to succeed.

Adam Smith's views are most appropriate here:

> The statesman that would attempt to direct private people in what manner they ought to employ their capitals, would not only load himself with a most unnecessary attention, but assume an authority which could safely be trusted to no council or senate whatever, and which could nowhere be so dangerous as in the hands of a man who had folly and presumption enough to fancy himself fit to exercise it.[7]

In an attempt to alleviate suffering and poverty, we must focus not only on the need of the recipients, but on the cause of the situation. In addressing structional and generational poverty, we must look toward reforming some of the most likely poor: prisoners.

The true have-nots in our society are the two million inhabitants of our prisons. The reform of prisons must be an immediate objective. Years ago, a local radio station aired a discussion regarding prison philosophy in the 1800's.[8] Three tenets used for treatment of inmates were: solitary confinement, physical labor and religious education. Solitary confinement allows one time to think about what he has done. It also removes the human being from others; a great need given that people are social animals. Physical labor repays the debt to society, which is owed for the crime committed. Religious education allows for the instruction of grace, mercy, faith and the understanding that you should do unto others as you would have others do on to you. Alexis De Tocqueville even wrote of the movement in the United States in the nineteenth century, which combined incarceration with reforming the individual.[9] I believe that this strategy has been lost due to new social theories or differentiating political viewpoints. We are failing. Most importantly, we are failing those who need our help.

We currently have a prison system void of these elements. Although there are many facilities that are maximum security, the number of repeat offenders demonstrates that an overhaul is needed. We must look even toward the most minor improvements in having 25,000 fewer return offenders in a two or three year period. From a financial standpoint, some crime is a time value of money calculation. Offenders make a decision that it is better to have something now that is free than to have to work for it and buy it later. This behavior has to be corrected in order to have the released prisoner become a productive citizen. Without instilling a sense of morality and connecting with the "better angels of our nature," reform without ethics will fail.

Human capital development is the most critical element in the long term success of a nation. Economically, long term growth is based on inputs (what you've got) and usage (how you use it). This applies not to material, but people. In order to remain globally competitive, with a domestically viable economy we must develop long term reform of social policies that have fostered dependency. Addressing the areas of healthcare, structural poverty and prison reform will assist in making the United States a more vibrant nation with a better human capital base. From a fiscal standpoint, we will be a healthier nation, as well. If we ignore these issues, we risk having our society regress even further.

CHAPTER 8
OUR ONLY WAY OUT

"Tell me this isn't a government operation."
Ed Harris, in Apollo 13

The current economic crisis may take place in four phases: 2008 financial; 2009 economic reaction; 2010 currency; 2011 taxation. The solution to this crisis will not be found by adding trillions of dollars in additional bank credits to the economy. Many sectors of the distorted economy must be allowed to bottom and failure will need to occur. The residential real estate market could bottom in 2010 with the commercial real estate market bottoming in 2011. Professionals in the commercial market believe that the United States is only half way through the deleveraging process. As the United States' national debt approaches its GDP, the dollar may weaken. If foreigners refuse to purchase our treasuries or sell them outright, there will be additional upward pressure on interest rates and downward pressure on our currency. If taxes are increased in 2011, a full economic recovery may not occur.

In attempting to solve the current economic crisis, we must look for solutions to past macroeconomic problems; turning to the printing press has never been one of the answers. A brief review of previous chapters is appropriate in order to present a historical perspective on how to solve our problems. Attention is warranted to what has and what has not worked.

The dismantling of the medieval guild system and the establishment of more open trade helped the world expand throughout the 1800's as many of Adam Smith's ideas from the *Wealth of Nations* were adopted. Much of the United States' economic success is due to free trade between the states, Smith's idea that is found in Article I, Section 9 of the U.S. Constitution. Adam Smith and the enlightened leaders of the time understood that the wealth of nations was not determined by the amount of gold in the vault, but by the division of labor, which trade and specialization enhances.

Smith also made it very clear that everyone acts in their own self interest and that one's innate self interest must be kept in check by religious guidelines or principles. Our generation has mastered the former and neglected the latter.

Gold has played a positive role in economic history although it has been the target of much blame and false accusations. In the late 1700's, runaway fiat inflation in France ended with the establishment of the gold standard. While at war, Napoleon vowed never to return to the printing press. The sale of Louisiana in 1803 for $15 million in gold helped him to make good on his promise. Article I, Section 10 of the U.S. Constitution mandates gold and silver for use as currency, for sound reasons. With the gold standard in place from 1821 to 1914 economies of the United States and Great Britain expanded. The U.S. left the standard to fund the Civil War and returned to it in 1879. Westward expansion continued for 35 years, with deflation.

Following the First World War, Germany's hyperinflation in the 1920's ended with gold being reintroduced. Although reparations bear much of the blame for the inflation, social spending did not help the situation.

After World War II, the Marshall Plan received the lion's share of credit for the German economic miracle. Credit must be shared with Ludwig Erhard, who, in June 1948, lifted wage and price controls and instituted the West German Deutsch Mark.

In more recent history, Ronald Reagan's first two executive orders were economically related: decontrolling crude oil and refined petroleum products and terminating Jimmy Carter's wage and price controls.[1] The long thaw from the 1970's had begun. His tax cuts reinvigorated the economy and gave individuals greater control over their own private property. We are now facing an economic crisis similar to the 1970's and the 1930's. It is a crisis of our own making and finds its roots in the expansion of credit.

The root of the word credit derives from Latin, *credere*, meaning to believe. Globally, no one knows what to believe. The United States Government and the Federal Reserve System bear most of the blame for the current economic crisis. The remainder of the blame can be assigned to many actors. Responsibility must be shared by individual consumers who were unable to resist the temptation of assuming too much debt in too short of time without the means to pay it back. Lenders were reckless, as were brokers, who sold loans with questionable value. The government played a part in the lending malfeasance as Fannie Mae and Freddie Mac, the quasi-public/private mortgage wholesalers, looked the other way. Insurance companies underwrote policies without having actual, as opposed to adequate, reserves to make good on their promise to pay. The difference being what was allowed according to models and regulation and what reserves were really needed. Again, there was no internal check on consumers' or businesses' own self interest. A rough timeline of most events in the financial crisis follows.

The crisis began early in the decade as the Federal Reserve began cutting interest rates. Holding the Federal Funds Rates at one percent from June 2003 until June 2004 distorted the financial system. Banks began easing lending standards with the goal that every American should own a home. No documentation "no doc" loans were common, with only verbal proof of earnings needed by the borrower. No income, no asset (NINA) loans were another type of security available. Finally, the no income, no job, or no asset (NINJA) loan really highlights the distorted nature of the lending sector. The acronym is most appropriate given the effect on the borrower, lender and the economy.

In March 2005, the "zero down" mortgage came into being and the financial perfect storm emerged: low interest rates, easy lending standards and no down payment required. During this time period lenders and brokers encouraged individuals to do cash out re-financing and plow assets into the equity markets. Cheap rates on your money and double digit returns in the market: a "no brainer." Mortgage and stock brokers concentrated on the returns and completely ignored the risk.

Lenders were able to package these risky loans and sell them to buyers on Wall Street. These buyers had no problem turning an easy profit as these loans, divided into different categories of debt, and were sold throughout the world on unsuspecting pension plans and hedge funds. We "slimed" the world with lousy paper, as one broker said. This debt achieved higher ratings due to the fact that it was insured by respected global insurance carriers.

One of these insurance carriers, AIG, purported to have plenty of assets to support potential claims on bad loans and unsuspecting customers learned too late as AIG went running for a bailout which went from $85 billion to $150 billion, then $180 billion. It is quite possible that AIG will be asking for and receiving more money, as they will have more claims in the future and very few assets to settle them.

The undoing of this entire situation began when the Federal Reserve began raising rates in June 2004. In only two short years, individuals who borrowed for a short term mortgage such as a one, three or five year adjustable rate mortgages (ARM's), began to incur higher payments. Rather than educating the public, the government and lenders took advantage of the ignorance of the public. Lenders should have encouraged businesses and consumers to lock their mortgages for the long term.

As people began to default on their mortgages, the amount of homes for sale exceeded the amount of buyers and prices began falling. As the income from the loans in default mounted, the value of the underlying securities began to drop. Insurance claims for securitized mortgages soared. Home values plummeted.

The Federal Reserve began aggressive open market operations in the summer of 2007 in reaction to the economic events. Alan Greenspan's mistake of cutting rates and holding them too low for too long would be repeated in September 2007. The Fed under Ben Bernanke began a moving to a target rate of zero to one quarter percent by December 2008.

Table 8.1

Selected Government Actions
2008-2009

2008	Program	Amount
Jan.-Dec.	Fed Injections	$1 trillion (est.)
Mar.	Bear Stearns	29 billion
Apr.	Fiscal Stimulus	150 billion
Sept.	Fannie/Freddie	200 billion
Sept.-Nov.	AIG Bailout	150 billion
Sept.	T.A.R.P.	700 billion
Oct.	Money Mkts./Comm. Paper	500 billion
Nov.	Citigroup/Credit Spt.	1.1 trillion

2009	Program	Amount
Feb.	Fiscal Stimulus	$787 billon
Mar.	Quantitative Easing	300 billion
Mar.	P.P.I.P.	750 billion
Mar.	T.A.L.F.	200 billion
Oct.	FY 2010 Budget	3.5 trillion (est.)

The list of government intervention is well known. In every case, individuals in two different administrations provided the same excuse, "We must take this action or the entire system will fail."

The Bear Stearns deal represented the first overt act known to the general public to bailout the collapsing financial system. Other actions taken during the summer and fall of 2007 were substantial, but not well known. Bear Stearns represented a classic "false dilemma" situation. We must buy this company at $2.00 per share, because there are no other alternatives. Policymakers eventually settled on $10.00 per share, but never let a situation develop where the company would have been purchased at fifty cents per share by an entity in the private sector. (An error of a price of 500% for the valuation of a business deal is unheard of).

One of the latest and largest policies is the passage of the February 2009 stimulus bill. If this $787 billion fiscal stimulus were to create three million jobs, the cost would be roughly $262,000 per job. Central planners viewed the $150 billion dollar Bush Administration stimulus as not enough, so they decided to spend more money. There are rumors of another stimulus for fall 2009.

The Federal Reserve and the Treasury cannot print enough money to or issue enough debt to solve this crisis. These government entities with their respective principals, well versed in the school of Keynesian economic thought, do not understand that the distortion created by the expansion of credit throughout the system cannot be corrected by further inflation of the banking system. Prices must fall downward for the economy to reach a state of equilibrium, where the supply of goods will meet the demand of qualified purchasers. For years, prices were artificially high; there must be a correction.

The collapse is top down and cannot be fixed by additional credit at the bottom. No one has adequately addressed the strain on the United States dollar that this additional credit expansion or debt will cause. Many financial professionals are historically skeptical whether the Federal Reserve can skillfully remove the excess credit they are injecting to "save the system." The Fed failed to do its job after the 2003-2004 expansion; how can it have more credibility now?

The entire global financial system is still very weak. Only market based solutions will ease the current crisis. Mark-to-market lending regulation has been amended. This decision had been recommended to the Bush Administration and opposed by a few individuals, especially at the Securities and Exchange Commission and the Department of Treasury who desired that transparency be maintained. This modification is an excellent first step in ensuring that the bank's balance sheet of loans not be marked down to the worst fire sale price at the end of any given month to meet regulatory requirements.

The FICA or payroll tax must be eliminated for one year. Federal assets must be sold and budgets must be cut to pay for this tax cut. This would be temporary since social security along with Medicare and Medicaid still represent an unfunded liability of roughly $60 trillion. Only the 6.2 percent social security tax withholding for employers and employees would be eliminated; the Medicare portion would remain. As social security is one of the only programs that is solvent, the lack of revenue would not weaken the dollar or add to the national debt. It would be a non-inflationary boost to the economy, encouraging saving and spending.

Although analysts who use models to attempt to predict human behavior disagree with this recommendation, the uptick rule on the short selling of stocks must be reinstated. For many years investors could not sell a stock short, i.e. sell a stock they did not own, unless the last trade for the stock was in an upward direction. Under the new law, someone could sell a stock as it was trading downward and add pressure to the downward direction. This may have attributed to some of the volatility during the last hour of trading in the October/November 2008 timeframe as any institution could pile on a stock on the way down, without having to wait for the next trade that closed higher.

Private property rights form one of the cornerstones of civil society. Having the banks foreclose on their customers, when many were sold loans under suspicious circumstances, should be postponed, on a case by case basis. Loans should be restructured by adding two years to all qualified loans and have the lender pay interest only for the next two years, keeping taxes and other costs in place. The entire loan must be repaid. If there is evidence that the borrower lied on his application or stated other falsehoods, then the program should not be made available for these individuals. The taxpayers should not subsidize undesirable behavior. As in business, profits and losses direct future behavior, if an individual acted irresponsibly society should not be forced to pick up the tab.

In accordance with existing law, the government should set a broad policy so the market can make decisions and move forward. Business despises uncertainty. There is an existing policy recommendation regarding housing and lending that should not be made law, as it would add to uncertainty rather than eliminate it.

The concept is known as cramming and it is a terrible idea. If a lender does not agree to "work out" a loan a judge may overrule the lender. In theory, this may sound like a good policy. The net effect is to place doubt in the mind of anyone buying the loan from the lender if it is sold or securitized. Investors or even first issuers of the loan will automatically question the reliability of the debt if any judge can interfere or worse, overrule the law of contract. Instituted by the Roman Republic, contract law has stood the test of time for two thousand years. Given the recent decisions by the Obama Administration favoring unsecured debtors over bondholders in the Chrysler reorganization, allowing judges to overrule lenders will further damage lender confidence at a time where confidence must be restored. Cramming would have a chilling effect on the market.

Adding time to the loan, rather than forcing the lenders to modify the loan by individual magistrates, is the best course of action. Good guidelines must come from the Federal Government that apply to eligible borrowers; otherwise the market will be faced with complete uncertainty as to which loans will be restructured and which ones will be interfered with by the courts.

Another idea is which must be opposed is that the government needs to artificially fix or manipulate interest rates. This proposal completely ignores how rates are established by the market.

Interest rates have three main components: supply and demand for loanable funds, default premium and inflation premium. The more funds available the less expensive the rate, the less available the more it is valued; the higher the rate. The default premium is calculated by the lender as the risk that the borrower will default on the loan. Some components can be calculated mathematically using statistical analysis to determine how many borrowers will default given certain income levels, etc. The inflation premium discounts future inflationary expectations and includes the risk that the central bank may monetize the debt. Creditors need to charge "inflation plus."

As long as we continue to have policymakers who are allowed to determine the short term fixed rate of interest, the Federal Reserve should target gold at the marginal cost of production. If the spot price of gold reaches above this level, rates should be raised. If gold drops below this level, rates should be lowered. Long term interest rates would drop immediately, as the inflation premium would be drastically reduced. Further, capital would move into the United States as monetary stability would be anticipated by global capital. We are in a period of daily uncertainty. This would remove some of the doubt, especially regarding the strength of the world's reserve currency.

On March 18, 2009, The Federal Reserve purchased $300 billion in thirty year treasuries to "drive" the yield of rates downward and make mortgages more affordable. This action only worked for roughly one month and then ten year treasury yield returned to its previous rate. The market fears inflation and there is nothing that twelve members of the Federal Open Market Committee can do except postpone the reckoning from errors in centralized planning. Targeting a specific price of gold would achieve the desired effect without further damaging the currency and causing inflation. As of May 27, 2009, the ten year Treasury bond yielded 3.51 percent and had moved over one half percent in a very short time period. In June, it would reach 3.996 percent. It is very possible that this yield could move over four percent, especially if foreigners refrain from purchasing treasuries.

The Federal Reserve should be prohibited from purchasing government debt. This behavior allows the government to live beyond its means and devalues the dollar. Whether engaging in open market operations or purchasing securities directly from the Treasury, the Fed should no longer be allowed to use these actions to print money and debauch the currency.

Savings should be encouraged, not discouraged. Savings is simply postponed spending. It is future oriented and this capital will be borrowed and used by business to become more efficient. Real savings reduces interest rates. If the banks need to be recapitalized, why not have the public provide this service than have the government print money and inject into the banking system, weakening the currency and driving up the national debt? If the government waived the income tax on interest earned, business and individuals would recapitalize the banks through increased savings, capital investments or dividends.

There is an often quoted "paradox of thrift," a Keynesian notion that savings is good for individuals, but bad for the economy as it reduces spending. Although 72 percent of GDP is comprised of consumer demand, the consumer does not know what he or she wants until they see it. The concept of Say's Law holds true: supply creates its own demand or in the popular vernacular from the movie, *Field of Dreams*, "If you build it, he will come." As Mark Skousen said, "It was Chrysler who invented the mini-van, it was the consumer that decided it needed a door on the left side." [2]

Politicians rarely campaign on a platform of making it easier for entrepreneurs to create jobs. Candidates brag about how many jobs they will create. A temporary reduction of taxes on interest and capital gains should be enacted. Reducing capital gains taxes will encourage the formation of capital.

The United States should institute unilateral free trade. Total receipts in fiscal year 2007 for customs duties and tariffs totaled $27 billion. [3] Foreign governments would respond in kind, lowering their tariffs and our exports would increase. Corporate tax revenue would exceed the lost tariff revenue, as American corporations would generate more revenue that would be taxed at a higher rate than imports. Companies and workers would gain, as would the federal government. The stock market would increase based on discounted higher future earnings.

In the early part of this decade, the market peaked two times post September 11, 2001, March 2002 and February 2004, based on steel tariffs and the export tax credit law. This mirrors the behavior of the market in October 1929 as the world learned that the Smoot Hawley Tariff bill would become law if not in the current session of congress, than in the next. Had the Bush Administration been more progressive in its trade policy and negotiations in the Doha Round of Trade, we may have been able to build a better base of prosperity, instead of one based on the false premise of easy credit.

An example of what not to do regarding trade is noted below. It is taken verbatim from the February 2009 stimulus bill and is part of the Buy American provision that has made our allies furious.

Section 1605

USE OF AMERICAN IRON, STEEL, AND MANUFACTURED GOODS

(a) None of the funds appropriated or otherwise made available by this Act may be used for a project for the construction, alteration, maintenance, or repair of a public building or public work unless all of the iron, steel, and manufactured goods used in the project are produced in the United States.

(b) Subsection (a) shall not apply in any case or category of cases in which the head of the Federal department or agency involved finds that—

(1) applying subsection (a) would be inconsistent with the public interest;

(2) iron, steel, and the relevant manufactured goods are not produced in the United States in sufficient and reasonably available quantities and of a satisfactory quality; or

(3) inclusion of iron, steel, and manufactured goods produced in the United States will increase the cost of the overall project by more than 25 percent.

(c) If the head of a Federal department or agency determines that it is necessary to waive the application of subsection (a) based on a finding under subsection (b), the head of the department or agency shall

publish in the Federal Register a detailed written   justification as to
why the provision is being waived.
(d) This section shall be applied in a manner consistent with United
States obligations under international agreements.[4]

Given the instructions found in paragraph (b) section (3), it would be
of no surprise to see costs increase twenty four percent above the normal
market price.

This bill became law in February 2009. By the end of May 2009,
representatives of twelve cities in Canada passed ordinances against buying American products. The European Union, Brazil, Canada, Japan and
Mexico are discussing possible responses to American protectionism.
Duferco Ferrell, an American Steel company, may have to lay off workers because some of its goods are produced abroad and imported into the
United States. Houston based Westlake Chemicals has lost sales to a Canadian vinyl pipe maker because they cannot bid for American jobs and
will cut orders from its American supplier.[5] This action eerily resembles
the actions of our allies following the passage of the Smoot Hawley Tariff on June 17, 1930.

The irony of this action by a "progressive" Administration is that the
last Democrat president understood trade. President Clinton turned his
back on his largest group of support, labor unions, to pass NAFTA and
GATT because he knew that free trade means jobs. He was reelected.

Adding insult to injury, the United States deliberately angered our
Mexican trading partners with the inclusion of this wording in House
Resolution 1105, the Omnibus Appropriations Act of 2009:

> None of the funds appropriated or otherwise made available under
> this act may be used, directly or to establish, implement, continue,
> promote, or in any way permit a cross border motor carrier demon-
> stration program to allow Mexican-domiciled motor carriers to oper-
> ate beyond the commercial zones along the international border be-
> tween the United States and Mexico, including continuing, in whole
> or in part, any such program that as imitated prior to the date of the
> enactment of this Act.[6]

When this bill became law the Mexican government retaliated on
March 18, 2009, viewing this as a violation of the NAFTA accords. The
Mexicans raised tariffs on 89 American products from 10 percent to 45
percent and U.S. products became more expensive and less competitive.[7]
Once again, American policymakers were reminded that in a global
economy, there is no such thing as a sovereign regulation.

Instead of a budget busting stimulus, the government must begin a reduction of at least ten percent of its workforce. This would mirror the anticipated national unemployment rate by the end of 2009. Currently the highest state unemployment rate is over fourteen percent in Michigan. The federal budget must be cut immediately and accordingly. Instead of adding to the federal deficit, it must be reduced. The only exception would be for national defense.

Defending the nation in time of war is expensive. We suffer human loss and a reallocation of our resources. Given the successes of our enemies in Iraq, Afghanistan and Pakistan, the war could last for decades. We should have a funding plan that includes selling assets and closing cabinet departments, channeling those assets into national defense.

Banks must return to lending as their primary function. Banks should no longer have a brokerage arm, offer investment advice or sell insurance. As everyone now understands, lending is a critical element in a market based system and it must be maintained with the highest standards of integrity. The old 3-6-3 rule was not so bad. Pay 3 percent in a savings account, charge 6 percent on a mortgage and be on the golf course by 3 pm. Tempted by easy credit and loose lending laws, banks and other lenders helped cause the bust by carelessly creating the boom. The government should regulate the banks and other lenders, instead of bailing them out. Some of the senior officials that spent all day communicating and not one minute thinking about the ramifications of their business deals should be investigated. Too many CEOs remain in charge of institutions that directly contributed to this meltdown.

Brokerage firms and investment banks should be completely separate. No longer should an investment banker in the firm be able to push a new issue on to a broker of the same firm. There has always been a conflict of interest in situations such as these, especially when higher commissions are paid in support of a new issue. To assume otherwise is to deny reality.

Tax increases in the year 2011 must be avoided. An increase will have the same effect as Hoover's tax increases in 1932. The economy will suffer a tremendous body blow, as remaining capital is taken from individuals and businesses to be spent less efficiently by government. Recall the Viking Yacht example and the Luxury Tax of 1990. The tax backfired.

It is not possible to add forty six million individuals to the rolls of healthcare with unrealistic projected tax receipts from the wealthiest Americans. If this course of action continues unabated, the United States will never recover. The timing could not be worse.

Removing the mortgage interest deduction on earners over $250,000 will result in the rich buying fewer large homes and all of the carpenters, plumbers and electricians who earn under $250,000 will be the most adversely affected. Phasing out charitable deductions for the highest income earners will result in fewer charitable contributions and the poor and needy will be the most affected. The market impact will be exactly the opposite of the intent of government policy. Beware of unenlightened benevolence.

It is ironic that the individuals who will be most responsible for the economic recovery, business owners, are being targeted for wealth redistribution. Many businesses in the United States are owner-operated sub chapter S corporations. Income flows directly to the owner's bottom line. Increase taxes on the business owner; he or she will lay off more employees to keep the going concern intact. A business owner knows more than anyone else and can operate only a few key employees.

Over the past few months, politicians and people on the street believe that the rich did too well during the Bush Administration. So the populist solution is to give everyone else the wealth that was earned by the top wage earners. The entrepreneurs and savers know how to earn it and most importantly, they understand how to preserve it. A vast majority of the wealth in the United States has been created by entrepreneurs. In the year 2000, 263 of the wealthiest 400 Americans, almost two-thirds, made their fortunes from scratch. Only nineteen percent on the Forbes list inherited their fortunes.[8]

There is a disconnect in the economy; banks are able to lend, but are not willing, and consumers are willing to borrow and are not able. Interest rates are now lower than they were in 2003-2004. This situation meets the definition of insanity: repeating the same behavior, expecting a different outcome. With the latest $787 billion injection into the financial system from the February 2009 stimulus, some Washington "whispers" place the total fiduciary credit placed since 2007 now at $10 trillion, more than three quarters of U.S. annual GDP, a frightening statistic. As this stimulus bill is brought forward, a weaker currency may be the result. There is even talk of a second stimulus in the fall, if this one fails to jump start the economy. There is a technical term that may be applied to this behavior: madness.

The market cannot be ignored. There was an "Obama Bounce" after the election, with the market bottoming around November 20th. Although the news continued to be negative, the market began to rise until early January, when the Administration announced its new plans to add to the debt, raise taxes, add forty million to the healthcare rolls, implement emissions standards on the auto makers, phase out interest and charitable deductions for high wage earners, impose cap and trade regulations, as well as a host of other programs. There was a reason the market was down twenty percent in the first six weeks since the President took office. This market performance cannot be blamed on inherited problems. The market is a leading economic indicator and is warning us about further troubles. As recently as March 13, 2009, senior Obama economic officials continued to embrace fiscal stimulus based on the fact that such policies worked in the Great Depression.[9]

We can and we must do better! Although the political parties have changed in Washington, the economics has not. Advancing along the lines of free trade, stable currency and private property rights is a good first step.

CHAPTER 9
HELP WANTED

"In order for evil to triumph, good men need do nothing."
Edmund Burke

"He who will not apply new remedies must expect new evils."
Sir Francis Bacon

On the evening of December 24, 1985, light snow fell at a small border camp in Weiden, West Germany. The American patrols were out, observing the Czechoslovakian frontier. Around 2100 hours the phone rang in "The Scrounge," the after hour movie room the soldiers stationed at the camp frequented. The gate guard called for the camp duty officer. I had that position for my unit's tour of duty. I answered the phone and was informed that a German Officer was at the front gate and desired to see the commander. I spoke the language and went to the gate. In the dim light I believed the officer to be a Major. We visited briefly and proceeded inside.

As we entered the building that housed The Scrounge, I noticed that the officer was not a major, but a brigadier general, the rank structure was the same, only the color was different. The officer was the commander of the German Kaserne across the street from us. I introduced him to my commander Captain Terry Wolff and he asked if he could address the men.

He gave a wonderful speech. He thanked us for being 8,000 miles from home and spending time away from our families defending his family and his country on Christmas Eve. He spoke of our strong alliance and partnership. He spoke of unity and shared values. He wished us all Merry Christmas and departed to a cheer of "Oohrah," an expression of happiness from the men. Terry and I walked him back to the gate and told him how grateful we were that he took time from his family to come to see us. We saluted and he returned it. I wished him Merry Christmas and Happy New Year in his own language. This was international relations at its finest.

This was only one small example of friendship, respect and trust that helped win the cold war. The fall of communism and the reopening of much of the world to trade, commerce and dialog was more a political event rather than an economic one. Sound economies and global prosperity should have been the result. But, as is true with most situations, we have solved old problems; new ones have taken their place. We face a world made more complicated by our recent economic crisis. This contagion has brought radical ideas to the forefront and calls for greater centralized control at national and international levels. These solutions will only complicate matters and increase problems between and within countries.

The greatest single source of global tension is the separation of wealth between haves and have-nots. This must be addressed through the opening of trading lanes to enable the developed nations to become even more specialized and the less developed nations to enhance their division of labor and raise their standard of living. There will be winners and losers on both sides of the ocean.

Winners include those whose goods and services are demanded by the market and who specialize in products and services. Individuals who have money invested in the bond and stock markets will benefit immediately as capital flows will increase, as will the future earnings of corporations. Corporate earnings will rise on the news that tariffs will be lifted, as markets discount future earnings. Consumers will benefit as prices of goods will decrease. Businesses will benefit as cost of inputs will decrease, lowering expenses. Savings will increase as a result, as individuals will have more disposable personal income.

Those who will not benefit include organizations that receive subsidies and industries that receive tariff or quota protections. Industries that are owed political favors would need to cut expenses and compete. Often those who belong to interest groups forget that they are also consumers. Consumers represent the only interest group in the world which everyone belongs, but no one has to join. We should always consider ourselves as consumers first and understand that relationship to the market before all others. Free trade benefits all consumers and leads to lower prices and higher profits.

The alternative to free trade is protectionism and economic nationalism, akin to the 1930's. This could result in a global conflict that could dwarf the Second World War, with the release of nuclear weapons a distinct possibility. This danger must be understood and prevented. Deterrence as a grand strategy has been successful as nations that opposed the United States valued human life, as did we. Should nuclear weapons fall into the hands of those who would rather perish than live, the world will face great peril. This issue can be addressed successfully without military force. We need to rapidly adopt policies which increase global wealth.

Following fifty years of public service, Secretary of State Cordell Hull wrote the following in his memoirs about the close relationship between trade and peace:

> "I saw that you could not separate the idea of commerce from the idea of war and peace. You could not have serious war anywhere in the world and expect commerce to go on as before. . . . And (I saw that) wars were caused by economic rivalry. . . . I thereupon came to believe that . . . if we could increase economic exchanges among nations over lowered trade and tariff barriers and remove international obstacles to trade, we could go a long way toward eliminating war itself."[1]

Even in the most popular science fiction movie series in history, *Star Wars*, trouble begins in a galaxy far away with a dispute over trade:

> Turmoil has engulfed the Galactic Republic. The taxation of trade routes to outlying star systems is in dispute. Hoping to resolve the matter with a blockade of deadly battleships, the greedy Trade Federation has stopped all shipping to the small planet of Naboo. While the Congress of the Republic endlessly debates this alarming chain of events, the Supreme Chancellor has secretly dispatched two Jedi Knights, the guardians of peace and justice in the galaxy, to settle the conflict. . . .[2]

Keeping the trading lanes open appears to be a wise decision in both the real world and that of fiction. In 5,000 years of recorded history, there has never been a case where someone being able to buy the best product at the lowest possible price hurt the overall well being of a nation. Free trade is the key for real peace. The increase of global wealth will be the best method of establishing an environment in which reasonable people can resolve differences. No one thinks very well when they are hungry and angry. From a national security standpoint, the best defense against terrorism is global prosperity. Historically, poverty and crisis are breeding grounds for false prophets.

The idea of conflict necessitating change and capitalism's demise into socialism resulting in a utopian communist state never materialized. In actuality, the exact opposite occurred. Despite the purges, centralized planning and police states, the communists only enriched a few percent, the ruling class, at the expense of the masses. Global capitalism carried the day. We now risk moving backward with policies of ignorance. We must glean wisdom from the past and assess which policies have worked best.

Possessing a basic understanding of how markets work is critical to comprehending how trade impacts future earnings on these markets. Most importantly, Adam Smith identified the mercantile system as a key factor in the lack of progress from 1500 to 1776. The concept of "beggar thy neighbor," I can trade with you, but you cannot trade with me, contributed to a world of economic stagnation. Trade and merchant guilds inhibited the development of the true specialization and depressed trade and exchange. Further contributing to a lack of progress was the belief that the wealth of a nation was determined by how much gold and silver was in the national vault, as opposed to its true determinate, its division of labor. Smith also concluded, "The most decisive mark of the prosperity of any country is the increase of the number of its inhabitants."[3] Nations with a negative or low population growth warn of future economic trouble. This is especially true when older citizens, who rely on social programs, outnumber younger citizens, whose taxes provide benefits to previous generations.

History demonstrates if we open the global trading lanes, markets will rise dramatically and much wealth will be created. A properly functioning market system can increase the standard of living. Rich and poor can benefit, without taking from one another to do so. It has been said that if you ask astronauts what they notice when they look back at the earth for the first time, most will respond, "No borders." We should take that attitude to the rest of the world with respect to trade.

The United States must unilaterally adopt free trade. Even if the world would only partially follow our lead, prices of goods and services would drop. The value of worldwide equity markets would increase based on the belief that future earnings would rise dramatically. In a pragmatic sense, if only marginal progress were made, many jobs would be created by a global increase of 2-3 percent of each nation's annual GDP. To quote Thomas Friedman, "Even as the world gets flat, America as a whole will benefit more by sticking to the principles of free trade, as it always has, than by trying to erect walls, which will only provoke others to do the same and impoverish us all."[4]

Regarding a specific trade policy, there is no greater signal that America can send to its partners than that of reducing or phasing out crop subsidies. Our overproduction of crops creates a global surplus and depresses prices overseas, creating poverty and situations where it is possible for radicals to come to and retain power. The failure of the Doha Round of GATT is a direct result of the developed world failing to lead by example. On many instances in the past several years, the lesser developed nations protested bitterly at the intransigence of the G-8 nations. We must act unilaterally and set an example for others to follow. Trade allows for prosperity and currency facilitates the transactions.

The United States must stabilize its currency, so the dollar is once again a store of value, rather than a target of speculation and arbitrage. When your parents sell their house, they will not get a house of equal size; they will buy a condo with the assets. There are more used cars sold than ever before and more cars are leased than purchased. Depriving people of their private property rights does not lead to a free society which enjoys liberty. Recognizing that the price of gold is an indicator of inflation is a good starting point. Gold has been incorrectly indicted as a cause of economic problems rather than being viewed as a useful tool which can provide needed information to policymakers. Gold has been convicted in the court of economics without ever having been afforded a trail.

Although viewed as an anachronism, gold provides a needed signal and does represent the market's true view. In a speech entitled, "Money, Gold and the Great Depression," presented on March 2, 2004, Dr. Benjamin Bernanke's affirmed the traditional argument that gold and tight monetary policy caused a market correction and the ensuing Great Depression and references Dr. Milton Friedman's argument.[5] Dr. Bernanke restated his beliefs during a nationally televised broadcast on Sunday, March 15, 2009. He recalled that his lessons learned from the Great Depression were that the central bank allowed the money supply to decrease and that the banks were allowed to fail. There was no mention of a collapse of global trade, the Smoot Hawley Tariff of 1930 or the Revenue Act of 1932.[6]

Both Bernanke and Friedman have reached accurate conclusions with incomplete information. Their beliefs either ignore or dismiss the fact that once the market understood that the Smoot Hawley Tariff would become law, the market crashed. The crash did not occur because of the gold standard, tight monetary policy or the actions of the Federal Reserve. The market, the human mind, anticipates future actions and discounts accordingly in either a positive or negative manner, when assessing the underlying present value of securities.

From 1929-1933, the money supply did contract by 33 percent, but this was due to a collapse of asset prices because of a lack of future earnings: an abundance of sellers and an absence of buyers that drove global asset prices further downward. Global trade during the same time period decreased 66 percent. The Depression ensued due to a collapse of global trade and the Revenue Act of 1932. Had Roosevelt lifted two laws, the depression may have ended. Until this is broadly understood and embraced, modern economic theory will remain beholden to the myths of the past rather than the realities on which human progress is built.

The Great Depression ended because of the stabilization of the currency, the lifting of wage and price controls and the reopening of the trading lanes. Attempting to curry political favor with tariffs or quotas is laced with peril. The trade deficit argument is often used but the lesson is the same: attempting to manipulate a balance sheet where double entry bookkeeping is used results in distortion, especially when government officials believe they are simply dealing with an income statement. Fact: imports are paid in full. They need not be balanced by exports. Trade is a transactional relationship and the international balance of payments is, by definition, balanced.

The incorrect conclusions from the Great Depression have made our current economic problems worse. No nation has turned to the printing press with success. This tactic has been attempted before. In November 1932, *The Wall Street Journal* ran a front page article praising the promise of an inflationary policy. The essay supported the idea that the economy would benefit from a weaker currency.

> Aided by easier credit, business and trade should be encouraged in its revival. Old debts would become less of an intolerable burden since dollars would be reasonably valued. That in brief, is the promise of the so-called inflation. By ordinary standards, it isn't inflation at all.[7]

It is ironic that Roosevelt did pursue an inflationary policy whose effects were diminished by 1937. The Bush and Obama Administrations with cooperation from the Bernanke Fed are attempting the similar policies as the Roosevelt Administration pursued some 70 years ago. From a practical standpoint, we have not progressed.

Inflation benefits debtors at the expense of creditors. The American government is the largest debtor. Who is harmed? Some argue that inflation increases prices and therefore creates wealth. This is incorrect, as the government is not the source of wealth; markets determine wealth. With the national debt increasing at $3.5 billion per day and the Treasury issuing debt more than 200 days in 2009, legislators in Washington are unable to recognize the danger, as they do not understand the effects. Sir John Templeton provided sage advice, "As the government begins to support a larger and larger percentage of the population, the result may be chaos, but it will not be deflation."[8]

We are helplessly witnessing a destruction of the currency. Although all nations have turned to the printing press, none has done so with the vigor and historical ignorance as the United States. As of this writing, in July 2009, the amount of fiduciary credit injected into the banking system is unprecedented. This action is well known to Austrian economists and the end result is predicted.

> Increases in the quantity of money and fiduciary media will not enrich the world or build up what destructionism has torn down. Expansion of credit does lead to a boom at first, it is true, but sooner or later this boom is bound to crash. Only apparent and temporary relief can be won by tricks of banking and currency. In the long run they must land the nation in profounder catastrophe. For the damage such methods inflict on national well-being is all the heavier, the longer people have managed to deceive themselves with the illusion of prosperity which the continuous creation of credit has conjured up.[9]

As we become more technologically advanced and historically detached, we ignore the wisdom of the ancients at great risk. Aristotle's views on currency mirror the Austrian warning. "If those who employ a currency system choose to alter it, the coins cease to have their value, and can no longer be used to procure the necessities of life."[10] Twenty three centuries later, the dangers of currency manipulation remain the same.

In the current economic crisis, every action by the government has followed a similar pattern with the same excuse, "If we don't act now, the entire system will fail." This rationale was used with the Bear Stearns deal and those that followed. Long term, if the destruction of the currency is the end result of this ignorance, what is the point of the policy? The most famous quotation from the Vietnam War is most appropriate, "In order to save the village, we had to destroy it." Correcting currency and trade matters are only the first steps. Taxation is next.

In an attempt to find a peaceful and prosperous path to move nations forward, a centralized grab for private property is not recommended. *Spreading wealth must not be accomplished through a redistribution scheme or taxation program.* Despite people's best efforts, these programs only exacerbate problems rather than resolve them.

The United States must move to a flat tax. Elimination of the current tax code, where the current system has been prostituted to special interests, is the first priority. In addition to the economic benefits of a new tax system, the United States will release human capital, especially in the fields of law and accounting. This will benefit the country enormously. After all, we have endeavored to make people experts in tax law. The opportunity cost is enormous. At the end of the day, this productivity can be better utilized in other fields. Further, a flat tax will reduce lobbying and corruption.

From the individual and corporate side, certainty will be established and the yearly tax changes made to repay campaign contributions or curry favor for the next election will be eliminated. If most individuals pay similar rates of taxation without deductions, than arguments concerning fairness will be eliminated. Key in this policy is Congress and the White House actually having the moral courage to pass a balanced budget. If members of the armed forces are willing to risk their lives to defend the nation, why won't Members of Congress risk their careers to do the right thing? There is no way around doing right.

Government expansion and increased taxation on job creators and higher wage earners is not the answer. Reining in spending is the answer. Fifty years ago, the government faced similar problems with an economic slowdown and spending. Raising taxes would not have helped. "By 1960, the last year of the Eisenhower Administration, confiscation of all incomes in excess of $25,000 would have yielded revenue for only ten more days of federal spending."[11] The Kennedy Administration cut taxes. With an economy in severe recession and tax increases on the horizon in 2011, historical wisdom is needed most. Other outlays must be trimmed. Health care and Social Security are a good starting point.

Health care needs less government, not more. From Republicans on the right to Democrats on the left, few understand that more government will add to costs and limit choice. Many are attempting to bribe their constituents with their own money, promising them more free government services. Third party payer must be addressed in order for proper price points to be established in the market. Providers will charge what the market will bear and with the consumer not paying the bill, the costs are skyrocketing.

Taxation of individuals not joining a government plan will make matters worse, as the current administration attempts to punish those exercising their right to decide what plan is best for them and their family. Should government levy taxes or fines on businesses for opting out of a government plan, business will stop offering health care benefits to its employees. Millions of additional citizens will join the ranks of the uninsured, forcing them on a government plan, increasing the burden on taxpayers.

Since the government has the ability to print money, health care providers can bill programs such as Medicare time and time again. Comparing the nation of Canada, with a population of thirty one million, to the United States with a population of over 300 million and attempting to bring a system similar to Canada's to this country is incomprehensible. Experts may disagree on the similarities or differences, but one item is certain: the government will be making decisions. Another system which requires attention is Social Security.

Social Security is an oxymoron. We are losing our security and there is nothing social about it. Bethlehem Steel should have warned us about legacy costs. In 2002, there were 12,000 workers supporting 130,000 retirees and dependents.[12] The problems that the big three automakers are now encountering with legacy costs, that resulted in two bankruptcies, provide additional foreshadowing for the United States with Medicare, Medicaid and Social Security within thirty years. Using accrual accounting, estimates of the unfunded liabilities of these programs by the year 2040 total $60 trillion. United States GDP is roughly $14 trillion and contracting. In June 2009, the national debt reached $11.4 trillion and is increasing at $3.5 billion per day. We cannot tax, borrow or print our way out of this mess. It is over.

In order to fund social security, we are paying double by way of our own 6.2 percent payroll tax and our employer's 6.2 percent matching tax. Effectively this is a tax on 12.4 percent of our own income and the system is still in need of additional revenue. Social security should be means tested. People should be eased off over time; forty years. Individuals should be offered a buyout, similar to large corporations who are in financial difficulty and offer incentives to their employees to retire early. Another option is voluntary self direction. An option would be to allow the government to keep all of the money someone has paid in exchange to completely opt out of the system and direct 6.2 percent of future income into a 401(k) plan with other salary deferrals. Depending on one's age, citizens may act on this proposal. It would direct future income streams away from the general fund, but it would ease the overall burden by lessening the number of individuals in the plan, whose future liabilities would be removed.

Another area for review is the increasing level of poverty in the United States. We can control the spread of poverty by ending the programs which perpetuate it. We must make a graduated scale so when people begin to work, they do not lose all of their benefits all at once. Remove this obstacle to upward mobility and eliminate the permanent stratification of our urban and rural poor. Further, if we want more of the populace to be employed, ease the burden on employers who hire them.

The United States government can be compared to a 233 year old house that is still standing, that has had seven generations of tenants, none of whom removed their personal belongings when they moved out. We need a national housecleaning. For Congress, it needs a financial physical. The Senate should revert to its original elected body, members being elected by the representatives of state government, as mandated by the Constitution. This would limit graft and corruption. There was a reason the "Upper House" was set up to be elected in this manner by constitutional authority. The framers knew better. The role of government is not to make the ship go faster; its role is to not let the ship tip over. We need fewer federal employees not additional ones. Smaller and limited government is better government.

A great example of lean administration is from the Civil War when in May 1864, General Ulysses S. Grant commanded some 533,000 men as General-in-Chief of the Union Army with a staff of fourteen officers. At the time, this was the staff that a commander of a division would have had at his disposal.[13] The smaller the government, the fewer people there are to be corrupted. With the jobless rates soaring into the millions, it is no time to take money from the economy to support hiring more federal officials. The public unemployment rate should mirror the national private sector unemployment rate.

We must export knowledge and respect. Following the fall of the Soviet Union, the Russians asked for our assistance in getting their economy to become more market driven. We sent the Internal Revenue Service to teach them how to collect taxes. We can do better. Many of the reforms in this book have focused on institutions and policies; there are two great examples of individual behavior to follow.

First, our leaders must be great listeners. This is a human trait that is not taught, but is most needed. Our greatest president may also have been one of our best listeners. Washington asked for and received inputs from junior officers during the Revolutionary War.[14]

Washington's final victory, Yorktown, was a French plan that had been suggested to him more than a year earlier. General Rochambeau recommended that Washington abandon his strategy of a fixed battle against the British at New York or Boston and instead move south to Virginia to trap Cornwallis against the sea with a blockade from the French navy commanded by Count de Grasse.[15] Not only can we see the wisdom of Washington's ability to listen, we see the brilliance of his being able to act on the information presented.

Second, as an analogy has been used to compliment Washington for listening, praise must be afforded to Adam Smith for not merely providing the correct answers in economics, but asking the right question: What made nations wealthy? Smith provided the world both answers and illumination, in a time, much like today, where wisdom was most needed. So many students in this day and age have been educated to reach the right conclusions; so few to ask the right questions.

It has been said that the world had four choices in the twentieth century: Hitler's Germany; Stalin's Russia; Tojo's Japan; and the United States. That being said, we have much work to do. The victory over false ideologies, domestically and internationally, can only be won intellectually by answering the three basic questions of economics: what to produce; how to produce it; and who gets what. The most critical element is who decides: consumers exercising their free will or a centralized group of decision makers? We must over turn the false hope of collectivism by reinforcing what socialists fear most: liberty and faith, because they place the individual at the forefront. After all, the Bill of Rights is about the rights of the individual.

The social science of economics, described as the science of choice, must cleanse itself of depression era theories that have poisoned the discipline for decades. Practical financial economics, based on historical success is needed most. For centuries, scholars believed that the world was flat. In medicine, physicians were beholden to the idea that all diseases were blood disorders and a cure could only be found by bleeding the patient. Many scientists thought it impossible to break the sound barrier. Today, the discipline of economics faces similar obstructions. Professors and presidential advisors alike subscribe to the arcane notions that savings is bad, imports must equal exports, the gold standard caused the Great Depression and the best method of ending a recession is for the government to print, borrow and spend money. This insanity must end.

What is needed most in economics is a rejection of classroom theory based on intellectually bankrupt philosophies. Modern economics must begin with the acceptance that free trade creates wealth, that sound money has always worked best and that private property rights provide incentive. A renaissance in economics must occur and it must begin with the citizenry. Rather than vilify markets for creating the world's problems, we should use markets to provide solutions. Markets have stood the test of time.

It is my sincere hope that this work will move you in some manner to become actively engaged in a positive process that will result in market based policies being not simply put into place, but embraced to move us forward to what Winston Churchill referred to as, "Broad sunlit uplands."[16] Abraham Lincoln said, "I am a firm believer of the people. If given the truth, they can be depended upon to meet any national crisis. The great point is to bring them the real facts."[17]

You have them.

NOTES

Chapter 1

1. The title of structure of production is borrowed from Mark Skousen's book bearing the same name. The type of model used has its genesis in Hayek's triangle regarding capital being produced.

2. David R. Breuhan, "Macroeconomic Impact of the Steel Tariffs, " A briefing to the United States International Trade Commission, Washington, D.C. June 19, 2003, 3.

3. See Executive Summary, Economy –Wide Effects, United States International Trade Commission, "Steel-Consuming Industries: Competitive Conditions With Respect To Steel Safeguard Measures" (Investigation No. 332-452), Volume III: Executive Summaries and Investigation No. 332-452 (Report and Appendices), Publication No. 3632, (Washington, DC: USITC, 2003), ix-x.

4. Colin Powell, *My American Journey* (New York: Ballantine Books, 1996), 320.

5. Online NewsHour, "President Bush Lifts Steel Tariffs to Avert Trade War," December 4, 2003, http://www.pbs.org/newshour/updates/steel_12-04-03.html (accessed 05/15/2009).

Chapter 2

1. Despite an exhaustive search, I am unable to determine the origin of this quotation. Closest ideas are from John B. Say and Milton Freidman.

2. The idea for this chart came from Six Key Systems in Market Economies and Organizations highlighted in: Wayne Gable and Jerry Ellig, *Introduction to Market Based Management* (Fairfax: Center for Market Processes, 1993), 15.

3. Jay Winik, *April 1865: The Month That Saved America* (New York: Perennial, 2002), 290, 315.

Chapter 3

1. Winston S. Churchill, *The Second World War*, vol. 1, *The Gathering Storm* rev. ed. (London: Cassell & Co., 1949), 6.

2. The exchange rate for $1.00 is listed as .000218 per billion marks, per note 4 in source, United States Department of Commerce, *Statistical Abstract of the United States, 1924,* Forty Seventh Number (Washington, DC: USGPO, 1925), 276.

3. Churchill, 21.

4. The most basic measurement of money supply data is M-1, comprised largely of demand deposits in commercial banks. This data shows large increases. Milton Friedman and Anna Jacobson Schwartz, *A Monetary History of the United States, 1867-1960* (Princeton: Princeton University Press, 1993), 710-711.

5. Harold Bierman, Jr. "The 1929 Stock Market Crash", http://www. eh. net/encyclopedia/?article=Bierman. crash (accessed 9/14/2005).

6. Benjamin S. Bernanke, "Money, Gold and the Great Depression. " Remarks at the H. Parker Willis Lecture in Economic Policy. (Speech, Washington & Lee University, Lexington, VA March 2, 2004), 7-8.   http://www. federalreserve. gov/boarddocs/speeches/2004/200403022/default. htm   (accessed 4/12/2004).

7. U. S. Department of State Fact Sheet, "*Smoot Hawley Tariff.*" http://www. state. gov/r/pa/ho/time/id/17606. htm (accessed 4/26/2005).

8. Jude Wanniski, *The Way The World Works* (New York: Basic Books, Inc., 1978), 124.

9. Ibid., 122, 129-141.

10. "Leaders Insist Tariff Will Pass," *New York Times*, October 28, 1928.

11. Ibid.

12. Ibid.

13. W. Michael Cox and Richard Alm, *The Fruits of Free Trade, 2002 Annual Report Reprint.* Federal Reserve Bank of Dallas (Dallas: Dallas Federal Reserve, 2003), 22.

14. Ibid.

15. Douglas A. Irwin and Randall S. Kroszner, "Log Rolling and Economic Interests in the Passage of the Smoot Hawley Tariff," A Paper presented at the Carnegie-Rochester Conference on Public Policy, Pittsburg, PA. November 10-11, 1995. Revised February 1996, Table 2.

16. Jim Powell, *FDR's Folly* (New York: Crown Forum, 2003), 43.

17. Ibid.

18. Ibid., 44.

19. Ibid., 44-45.

20. Ibid., 45.

21. U.S. export data from the National Bureau of Economic Research. http://www.nber.org/databases/macrohistory/contents/chapter07.html See m07023, U.S. total exports 07/1866-10/1969. (accessed 7/12/2005).

22. U.S. monthly import data from the National Bureau of Economic Research. http://www.nber.org/databases/macrohistory/contents/chapter07.html See m07028, U.S. total imports 07/1866-10/1969. (accessed 7/12/2005).

23. *The New Encyclopedia Britanica*, 15th ed. Vol. 21, s. v. "The Economic Blizzard," 832.

24. Jim Powell, 43. Further referenced as Powell.

25. U. S. Department of State Fact Sheet, "Smoot-Hawley Tariff."

26. *Global Strategy Weekly*, Societe Generale, Cross Asset Research. January 15, 2009, 7.

27. *Tariff Act of 1930*, Public Law 361, 71st Cong., 2nd sess. (June 17, 1930), 590.

28. United States Bureau of the Census, *The Statistical History of the United States from Colonial Times to the Present* (Stanford, Conn: Fairfield Publishers: 1965), 712.

29. Powell, 84.

30. Friedman and Schwartz, 10-11.

31. Lawrence W. Reed, *Great Myths of the Great Depression* (Midland, MI: Mackinac Center, 2000), 7.

32. Ibid., 10.

33. Powell, 117.

34. Ibid.

35. Ibid. , 121.

36. Evan Wagshul, letter to the editor, *Wall Street Journal*, March 27, 2009.

37. Murray N. Rothbard, "The New Deal and the International Monetary System," *Watershed of Empire: Essays on New Deal Foreign Policy.* Ed. Lenard P. Liggio and James J. Martin. (Colorado Springs, CO: R. Myles, 1976), 36.

38. Ibid.

39. Ibid., 41.

40. Powell, ix.

41.Burton W. Folsom, Jr. "Do We Need a New New Deal?" *Imprimis,* Hillsdale College, January 2009, 4.

42. Powell, 67.

43. Ibid., 45.

44. Carolyn Dimitri, Anne Effland and Neilson Conklin, "The 20th Century Transformation of U. S. Agriculture and Farm Policy, " Electronic Information Bulletin Number 3, June 2005, 2. http://www. ers. usda. gov/publications/eib3/eib3. htm (accessed 11/10/2008).

45. Powell, 195.

46. Fair Labor Standards Act, http://en. wikipedia. org/wiki/Fair_Labor Standards_Act (accessed 11/13/2006).

47. Historical Debt Outstanding-Annual, 1900-1949. http://www. public-debt. treas. gov/opd. /opdhist03. htm (accessed 2/27/2001).

48. *The Statistical History of the United States*, Unemployment, Chart D46-47, 73.

49. "U. S. Presidents Ranked from Best to Worst," *Detroit Free Press*, November 17, 2000.

50. Bernanke, speech, 2.

51. Folsom, 4-5.

52. Michael M. Grynbaum, "Going for the Gold in Doom and Gloom," *New York Times*, October 27, 2008.

53. Regarding Eisenhower's trip from France to Russia following VE day, I remember this from a lecture at West Point but cannot find this in written form.

54. *Year by Year*, The History Channel, October 2, 1996.

55. Ibid.

56. United States Bureau of the Census, *Statistical Abstract of the United States: 1997,* 117th ed. , (Washington, D C: 1997), 332.

57. Brink Lindsey, *Against the Dead Hand* (New York: John Wiley & Sons, Inc.), 94.

58. Michael B. Lehmann, *The Irwin Guide to Using the Wall Street Journal, 7th ed.* (New York: McGraw-Hill, 2005), 177.

59. Llewellyn H. Rockwell, Jr. "Remarks at the State of the Union Symposium, " (Speech, Walsh College, Troy, MI, April 23, 2005).

60. *Public Papers of the Presidents, Harry S. Truman*, 1946. "Statement by the President upon terminating Price and Wage Controls." November 9, 1946. http://www. trumanlibrary. org/trumanpapers/pppus/1946/249. htm (accessed 6/3/2003).

61. Benjamin M. Anderson, *Economics and the Public Welfare*, 2nd ed.(Indianapolis: LibertyPress, 1979), 387.

62. Lindsey, 94.

63. Ibid., 92.

Chapter 4

1. Attributed to either Adam Smith or David Ricardo. Notes from graduate school, Walsh College, 1993.

2. Milton Friedman, *Capitalism and Freedom* (Chicago: The University of Chicago Press, 1982), 170.

3. United States Constitution, Article I, Section 9.

4. Meg Bortin, "French give Spielberg an earful about 'Ryan'," *Milwaukee Journal Sentinel*, September 9, 1998. http://findarticles.com/ (accessed 7/2/2007).

5. Ibid.

6. Donmoyer, Ryan J. "Ballmer Says Tax Would Move Mircosoft Jobs Offshore," http://www.bloomberg.com?apps/news?pid=20601087&sid=aAKluP7 yIwJY(accessed 6/3/2009).

7. Paul Cook made these remarks at a lecture at the Townsend Hotel in Birmingham, Michigan. Time period is 1998-2000. I attended the event.

8. This diagram has no title source and was a handout from a graduate course in the Department of Finance and Economics at Walsh College. The date was April 1994. Copyright is credited to the Federal Reserve Bank of Chicago.

9. Paul Strathern, *A Brief History of Economic Genius* (New York: Texere, 2002), 2.

10. John Steele Gordon, *An Empire of Wealth* (New York: HarperCollins, 2004), 9.

11. Greg Robb, "Trade Gap Grows as Oil Costs Offset Export Strength," *Wall Street Journal*, March 12, 2008.

12. David R. Breuhan, "Free trade aids stock prices, consumers," *Crain's Detroit Business,* January 24, 2005.

13. Roger Thurow and Scott Kilman, "Hanging by a Thread," *Wall Street Journal*, June 26, 2002.

14. Roger Thurow, et. al. "How an Addiction to Sugar Subsidies Hurts Development," *Wall Street Journal,* September 16, 2002.

15. British Broadcasting Corporation, *BBC World News*, March 29, 2007.

16. Arvind Subramanian, "A Farwell to Alms," *Wall Street Journal*, August 22, 2007.

17. Lindsey, 219.

18. Adam Smith , *An Inquiry into the Nature and Causes of the Wealth of Nations*, vol. 1. Ed. R. H. Campbell and A. S. Skinner (Indianapolis: LibertyClassics, 1981), 457. Reprinted from the Oxford Press edition, 1976.

Chapter 5

1. N. Gregory Mankiw, *Principles of Economics* (Fort Worth: The Dryden Press, 1998), 600-604.

2. The Federal Reserve, *The Wall Street Journal Guide to Understanding Money & Markets*(New York: AccessPress,1990), 104-105.

3. Federal Open Market Committee, Board of Governors of the Federal Reserve System, http://www.federalreserve.gov/monetrypolicy/fomc.htm (accessed 7/6/2009).

4. Ibid.

5. Gordon, 114.

6. Michael David Bordo, "The Classical Gold Standard: Some Lessons for Today, " *The Review*, Federal Reserve Bank of St. Louis, May 1981, 90. Taken

from Joseph G. Kvasnicka, Federal Reserve Bank of Chicago *Readings in International Finance*, third ed. 1986.

7. Judy Shelton, "Capitalism Needs a Sound-Money Foundation," *Wall Street Journal*, February 12, 2009.

8. Robert Higgs, *Crisis and Leviathan* (New York: Oxford University Press, 1987), 79.

9. David R. Breuhan, "National debt on pace to reach GDP," *Crain's Detroit Business*, August 28, 2006.

10. Table 1 data are as follows. If September 30th were on a weekend, the price reflects the close on Friday. National Debt Figures taken as of fiscal year end. Treasury Direct. Historical Debt Outstanding Annual 2000-2007. http://www. treasurydirect. gov/NP/NPGateway (accessed 11/13/2008).

11. Prices of gold accessed from Kitco Bullion Dealers Website. http://www.kitco.com/scripts/hist_charts/daily_graphs.cgi(accessed11/13/2008). New York spot price at close of day or indicated as last trade.

12. Oil data: U. S. Energy Information Administration, Cushing, OK Spot Price FOB . http://www. tonto. eia. doe. gov/dnav/pet/hist/rwtcd. htm (accessed 11/13/2008).

13. Exchange rates: http://www. x-rates. com/cgi-bin/hlookup. cgi (accessed 11/13/2008).

14. Fed Funds rate from Federal Reserve Bank of New York, http://ftp. ny. frb. rg/markets/statistics/dlyrates/fedrate. html (accessed 11/13/2008).

15. Chart idea format obtained from http://www. stockcharts. com (accessed 4/20/2007).

16. Susan Pulliam and Karen Richardson, "Buffett Unplugged: Hands-Off Managing, by Gut," *Wall Street Journal*, November 12-13, 2005.

17. Chart idea format obtained from http://www. stockcharts. com (accessed 3/20/2008).

18. Friedman, 41.

19. Mark Skousen, "Milton Friedman's Last Lunch," Forbes.com, http://www.forbes.com/forbes/2006/1211/056a_print.html (accessed 6/25/2009).

20. Smith, 43.

21. Hans F. Sennholz, *Age of Inflation* (Belmont, MA: Western Islands, 1979), 32.

22. Andrew Batson, Andrew Browne and Michael M. Phillips, "U. S. Insists China Fears Over Debt Unfounded," *Wall Street Journal*, March 14-15, 2009.

23. Ibid.

24. John Tanner, Member of Congress, Remarks to the House of Representatives, C-Span, February 14, 2006.

25. John Markoff, "2nd Big Bank sets I. O. U. Deadline For California," *New York Times*, July 24, 1992. http://query. nytimes. com/gst/fullpage. html?res=9E0CE3D810F937. . . (accessed 11/28/2007).

26. Sennholz, 174.

27. Harriet F. Cane, "Minimum Wage: Who Pays?" *Wall Street Journal*, March 13, 1998.

28. David Ranson and Penny Rusell, "In Gold We Trust," *Wall Street Journal*, May 18, 2006.

29. United States Constitution, Article I, Section 10.

30. Ludwig von Mises, *Socialism* (Indianapolis: LibertyClassics, 1979), 449.

31. Paul Johnson, "Let Economies Cure Themselves," *Forbes*, September 1, 2008, 27.

32. Ibid.

Chapter 6

1. Viking Yachts History, http://www. vikingyachts. com/main/history. asp (accessed 7/2/2007).

2. "Good Riddance to the Luxury Tax," *Wall Street Journal*, January 16, 2003.

3. Thomas Sowell, *The Vision of the Anointed* (New York: BasicBooks, 1995), 82.

4. Powell, 78.

5. Sowell, 211.

6. Larry Reed has many principles or maxims. He presented this at a State of the Union Symposium in 2000 or 2001 at Walsh College in Troy, Michigan.

7. Paul Veryser, "Manufacturing: Requirements for Recovery," (Lecture, the University of Detroit Mercy, Sterling Hts. MI. November 1, 2008).

8. Mark Skousen mentioned this to me on March 3, 2001, at dinner with Harry Veryser, Terry Davis, Joe Weglarz and Don Byrne.

9. NBC Television, *NBC Nightly News*, November 17, 1994.

Chapter 7

1. Milton Friedman may have made these remarks on the Larry King show in the early to mid 1990's. A search revealed no leads. I watched the program.

2. ABC Television, *Good Morning America,* August 21, 2007.

3. "National Health Preview," *Wall Street Journal*, March 27, 2009.

4. Supplemental Social Security, SSA Publication No. 05-11000, June 2007. http://www.ssa.gov.pubs/11000.html (accessed 7/11/2009).

5. Mark Haveman and Lynn Edward Reed, " Disincentives to Earn: An Analysis of Effective Tax Rates on Low Income Minnesota Households," (St. Paul: Minnesota Center for Public Finance Research, 2007), i.

6. Ibid.

7. F. A. Hayek, *The Road to Serfdom* (Chicago: University of Chicago Press, 1972), 56.

8. The information may have been presented on National Public Radio in the early 1990's. An on line search with NPR only archives programs to 1996. I listened to the program and recorded the notes.

9. Alexis de Tocqueville, *Democracy in America*, vol. 1, (New York: Vintage Books, 1990), 258.

Chapter 8

1. Executive Order 12287 and 12288, Executive Orders Disposition Tables,RonaldReagan-1981, http://www.archives.gov.federal_register/executive _orders_/1981_reagan.html (accessed 6/2/2003).

2. Mark Skousen, "Remarks at the State of the Union Symposium," (Walsh College, Troy, MI, March 3, 2001).

3. Historical tables of the Federal Budget. http://www. gpoaccess. gov/usbudget/fy09/browse. html (accessed 2/11/2009). Courtesy, Dan Miller, Senior Economist, Republican Staff on the Joint Economic Committee, United States Congress.

4. *American Recovery and Reinvestment Act of 2009,* Public Law No. 111-5, 111th Congress, 1st. Sess., (February 17, 2009), 189.

5. *New York Times*, "The Peril of 'Buy American'," June 3, 2009.

6. The Omnibus Appropriations Act of 2009, HR 1105, 111th Congress, 1st. sess. (January 6, 2009), 409. Courtesy Adam Pradko, Office of Dave Camp (R-MI).

7. "Mexico Retaliates," *Wall Street Journal*, March 19, 2009.

8. Gordon, 418.

9. "While Everyone Fiddles," *New York Times*, March 13, 2009.

Chapter 9

1. Pietra Rivoli, Ph. D. *The Travels of a T-Shirt in the Global Economy*, (New York: John Wiley & Sons, 2005), 214.

2. *Star Wars, Episode I, The Phantom Menace*, Lucasfilm Ltd., Twentieth Century Fox, copyright 2001.

3. Smith, 87-88.

4. Thomas. L. Friedman, *The World is Flat: A Brief History of the Twenty-First Century*, rev. ed. (New York: Farrar, Strauss and Giroux, 2006), 263.

5. Bernanke, speech.

6. Benjamin S. Bernanke, CBS Television, "The Chairman," *60 Minutes*, March 15, 2009.

7. Bernard Kilgore, *Wall Street Journal*, "Does Inflation Offer Promise?" November 5, 1932.

8. Sir John Templeton had many maxims. In the 1990's, this was presented by a Franklin Templeton representative at a luncheon at Gregory J. Schwartz & Co, Inc..

9. Von Mises, 449-450.

10. Aristotle, *The Politics*, rev. ed. (London: Penguin Books, 1981), 83.

11. Sennholz, 63.

12. Eduardo Porter, "Reinventing the Mill," *New York Times*, October 22, 2005. http://query.nytimes.com/fullpage.html?res... (accessed 5/28/2009) .

13. Major General J. F. C. Fuller, *Grant and Lee: A Study of Personality and Generalship* (Bloomington: Indiana University Press, 1982), 73.

14. Joseph Ellis, *His Excellency George Washington* (New York: Alfred A. Knopf, 2004), 175, 176.

15. Ibid., 133.

16. Winston S. Churchill, Address to the House of Commons, June 18, 1940.   http://www.loc.gov/exhibits/churchill/images/wc0104_ls.jpg   (accessed 5/21/2009).

17. Martin W. Sandler, *Lincoln Through the Lens: How Photography Revealed an Extraordinary Life* (New York: Walker & Company, 2008), 2.

REFERENCES

ABC Television. *Good Morning America.* August 21, 2007.

American Recovery and Reinvestment Act of 2009. Public Law No. 111-5. 111th Congress, 1st sess. February 17, 2009.

Anderson, Benjamin M. *Economics and the Public Welfare.* 2nd ed. Indianapolis, LibertyPress, 1979.

Aristotle. *The Politics.* Rev. ed. London: Penguin Books, 1981.

Batson, Andrew, Andrew Browne and Michael M. Phillips. "U.S. Insists China Fears Over Debt Unfounded." *Wall Street Journal,* March 14-15, 2009.

Bierman, Harold, Jr. "The 1929 Stock Market Crash." http://www.eh.net/encyc lopedia/?article=Bierman.crash (accessed 9/14/2005).

British Broadcasting Corporation. *BBC World News,* March 29, 2007.

Bernanke, Benjamin S. "Remarks at the H. Parker Willis Lecture in Economic Policy." Speech. Lexington, VA, March 2, 2004.

———Interview. CBS News, "The Chairman," *60 Minutes,* March 5, 2009.

Board of Governors of the Federal Reserve System. Federal Open Market Committee. http://www.federalreserve.gov/monetarypolicy/fomc.htm (accessed 7/6/2009).

Bordo, Michael David. " The Classical Gold Standard: Some Lessons for Today." *The Review.* Federal Reserve Bank of St. Louis, May 1981. From *Readings in International Finance,* 3rd. edition. Federal Reserve Bank of St. Louis, Ed. Joseph G. Kvasnicka, 1986.

Bortin, Meg. "French give Spielberg an earful about 'Ryan.'" *Milwaukee Journal Sentinel,* September 9, 1998. http://findarticles.com/ (accessed 7/2/2007).

Breuhan, David R. "Free Trade Aids Stock Prices, Consumers." *Crain's Detroit Business,* January 24, 2005.

———"Macroeconomic Impact of the Steel Tariffs." Presentation to the United States International Trade Commission, Washington, D.C. June 19, 2003.

———"National Debt on Pace to Exceed GDP." *Crain's Detroit Business,* August 28, 2006.

Cane, Harriet F. "Minimum Wage: Who Pays?" *Wall Street Journal,* March 13, 1998.

Churchill, Winston S. *The Second World War.* Vol. I, *The Gathering Storm.* rev. ed. London: Cassell & Co., 1949.

————Address to the House of Commons. June 18, 1940. http://www.loc.gov/exhibits/churchill/images/wc0104_ls.jpg (accessed 5/21/2009).

Cox, W. Michael and Richard Alm. *The Fruits of Free Trade, 2002 Annual Report Reprint, Federal Reserve Bank of Dallas.* Dallas: Dallas Federal Reserve, 2003.

Detroit Free Press, "U.S. Presidents Ranked from Best to Worst," November 17, 2000.

de Tocqueville, Alexis. *Democracy in America.* Vol 1. New York: Vintage Books, 1990.

Dimitri, Carolyn, Anne Effland and Neilson Conklin. "The 20th Century Transformation of U.S. Agriculture and Farm Policy." Electronic Information Bulletin Number 3, June 2005. http://www.ers.usda.gov/publications/eib3/eib3.htm (accessed 11/10/2008).

Donmoyer, Ryan J. "Ballmer Says Tax Would Move Mircosoft Jobs Offshore" (Update 1). Bloomberg.com http://www.bloomberg.com?apps/news?pid =20601087&sid=aAKluP7yIwJY (accessed 6/3/2009).

Ellis, Joseph J. *His Excellency George Washington.* New York: Alfred A. Knopf, 2004.

Exchange Rate Data. http://www.x-rates.com/cgi-bin/hlookup.cgi (accessed 11/13/2008).

Executive Order 12287 and 12288. Executive Orders Disposition Tables, Ronald Reagan_1981. http://www.archives.gov.federal_register/executive_orders /1981_reagan.html (accessed 6/2/2003).

Fair Labor Standards Act. http://en.wikipedia.org/wiki/Fair_Labor_Standards _Act (accessed 11/13/2006).

Federal Reserve Bank of New York. http://ftp. ny. frb. rg/markets/statistics/dly rates/fedrate. html (accessed 11/13/2008).

Friedman, Milton. *Capitalism and Freedom.* Chicago: The University of Chicago Press, 1982.

Friedman, Milton, and Anna Jacobson Schwartz. *A Monetary History of the United States.* Princeton: Princeton University Press, 1993.

Friedman, Thomas L. *The World is Flat: A Brief History of the Twenty-First Century.* Rev ed. New York: Farrar, Strauss and Giroux, 2006.

Fuller, Major General J.F.C. *Grant and Lee A Study of Personality and Generalship.* Bloomington: Indiana University Press, 1982.

Folsom, Burton W., Jr. "Do We Need a New New Deal?" *Imprimis.* Hillsdale College, January 2009.

Gable, Wayne and Jerry Ellig. *Introduction to Market-Based Management.* Fairfax: Center For Market Processes, 1993.

Gordon, John Steele. *An Empire of Wealth.* New York: HarperCollins, 2004.

Grynbaum, Michael M. "Going for Gold in Gloom and Doom," *New York Times*, October 27, 2008.

Haveman, Mark and Lynn Edward Reed, "Disincentives to Earn: An Analysis of Effective Tax Rates on Low Income Minnesota Households." (St. Paul: Minnesota Center for Public Finance Research, 2007.

Hayek, F.A. *The Road to Serfdom*. Chicago: The University of Chicago Press, 1972.

Higgs, Robert. *Crisis and Leviathan*. New York: Oxford University Press, 1987.

Historical Tables of the Federal Budget. http://www. gpoaccess.gov/usbudget /fy09/browse. html (accessed 2/11/2009).

Irwin, Douglas A. and Randall S. Kroszner. "Log-Rolling and Economic Interests in The Passage of the Smoot Hawley Tariff." A Paper Presented at the Carnegie-Rochester Conference on Public Policy, Pittsburg, PA. November 10-11, 1995. Revised February 1996.

Johnson, Paul. "Let Economies Cure Themselves." *Forbes*. September 1, 2008.

Kilgore, Bernard. "Does Inflation Offer Promise?" *Wall Street Journal*. November 5, 1932.

Kitco Bullion Dealers. Fiscal Year End Gold Prices. http://www.kitco.com /scripts/hist_charts/daily_graphs.cgi (accessed 11/13/2008).

Lehmann, Michael B. *The Irwin Guide to Using the Wall Street Journal*. 7th Ed. New York: McGraw Hill, 2005.

Lindsey, Brink. *Against The Dead Hand*. New York: John Wiley & Sons, Inc., 2002.

Mankiw, N. Gregory. *Principles of Economics*. Forth Worth: Dryden Press, 1998.

Markoff, John. "2nd Big Bank Sets I.O.U. Deadline For California." *New York Times*, July 24, 1992. http://query.nytimes.com/gst/fullpage.html?res= 9EOCED81031F937 (accessed 11/28/2007).

National Bureau of Economic Research. http://nber.org.databases/macrohistory /contents/chapter07.html (accessed 7/12/2005).

NBC News. *Meet the Press*. August 20, 2006.

——— *NBC Nightly News*. November 17, 1994.

New York Times. "Leaders Insist Tariff Will Pass," October 28, 1929.

——— "While Everyone Fiddles," March 13, 2009.

——— "The Peril of 'Buy American,'" June 3, 2009.

Online NewsHour. "President Bush Lifts Steel Tariffs to Avert Trade War." December 4, 2003. http://www.pbs.org/newshour/updates/steel_12-04-03.html (accessed 05/15/2009).

Public Papers of the Presidents, Harry S. Truman, 1946. "Statement of the President upon terminating Price and Wage Controls." November 9, 1946. http://www.trumanlibrary.org/trumanpapers/ppus/1946/249.htm (accessed 6/3/2003).

Powell, Colin. *My American Journey*. New York: Ballantine Books, 1996.

Powell, Jim. *FDR's Folly*. New York: Crown Forum, 2003.

Pulliam, Susan and Karen Richardson. "Buffett Unplugged: Hands off Managing by Gut." *Wall Street Journal*, November 12-13, 2005.

Porter Eduardo. "Reinventing the Mill." *New York Times*. October 22, 2005. http://query.nytimes.com/gst.fullpage.html?res... (accessed 5/28/2009).

Ranson, David and Penny Russell. "In Gold We Trust." *Wall Street Journal*, May 18, 2006.

Reed, Lawrence W. *Great Myths of the Great Depression*. Midland, MI: Mackinac Center for Public Policy, 2000.

Rivoli, Pietra, Ph.D. *The Travels of a T-Shirt in the Global Economy*. New York: John Wiley & Sons, Inc. 2005.

Robb, Greg. "Trade Gap Grows as Oil Costs Offset Export Strength." *Wall Street Journal*. March 12, 2008.

Rockwell, Llewellyn H. Jr. "Remarks at the State of the Union Symposium." Walsh College, Troy, MI. April 23, 2005.

Rothbard, Murray N. "The New Deal and the International Monetary System," *Watershed of Empire: Essays on New Deal Foreign Policy*. Ed. Lenard P. Liggio and James J. Martin. Colorado Springs: R. Myles, 1976.

Sandler, Martin W. *Lincoln Through the Lens: How Photography Reveled an Extraordinary Life*. New York: Walker & Company, 2008.

Sennholz, Hans F. *Age of Inflation*. Belmont, MA: Western Islands, 1979.

Shelton, Judy. "Capitalism Needs a Sound-Money Foundation." *Wall Street Journal*, February 12, 2009.

Skousen, Mark. "Milton Friedman's Last Lunch." Forbes.com. December 11, 2006. http://www.forbes.com/forbes/2006/1211/056a_print.html (accessed 06/25/2009).

———— "Remarks at the State of the Union Symposium." Walsh College, Troy, MI. March 3, 2001.

Smith, Adam. *An Inquiry into the Nature and Causes of the Wealth of Nations*. Vol.1. Ed. R.H. Campbell and A.S. Skinner. Liberty Press: Indianapolis, 1981. Reprinted from the Oxford University Press, 1976.

Sowell, Thomas. *The Vision of the Anointed*. New York: BasicBooks, 1995.

Social Security Administration. Supplemental Social Security Income, SSA Publication No. 05-11000, June 2007. http://www.ssa.gov.pubs/11000.html accessed (7/11/2009).

Star Wars, Episode I, The Phantom Menace. Lucasfilm Ltd. Twentieth Century Fox, copyright 2001.

Strathern, Paul. *A Brief History of Economic Genius*. New York: Texere, 2002.

Subramanian, Arvind. "A Farewell to Alms." *Wall Street Journal*, August 22, 2007.

Tanner, John, Member of Congress. "Remarks to the House of Representatives."C-Span, February 14, 2006.

Tariff Act of 1930. Public Law 361. 71st Cong., 2nd Session. June 17, 1930.

The History Channel. *Year by Year*. October 2, 1996.

The Wall Street Journal Guide to Understanding Money & Markets. New York: AccessPress, 1990.

Thurow, Roger, et. al. "How an Addiction to Sugar Subsidies Hurts Development." *Wall Street Journal*, September 16, 2002.

Thurow, Roger and Scott Kilman. "Hanging by a Thread." *Wall Street Journal.* June 26, 2002.

United States Bureau of the Census. *Statistical Abstract of the United States: 1997.* 117th ed. Washington, DC: USGPO, 1997.

United States Bureau of the Census. *The Statistical History of the United States from Colonial Times to the Present.* Stanford, Conn: Fairfield, 1965.

United States Congress. House. The Omnibus Appropriations Act of 2009. HR 1105. 111th Cong., 11th. sess. (January 6, 2009), 409.

United States Department of Commerce. *Statistical Abstract of the United States, 1924.* Forty Seventh Number Washington, DC: USGPO, 1925.

United States Department of State. "Smoot Hawley Tariff." http://www.state.gov/r/pa/ho/time/id/17606.htm (accessed 4/26/2005).

United States Department of Treasury. Historical Debt Outstanding-Annual 1900-1949. http://publicdebt.treas.gov/opd./opdhist03.htm (accessed 2/27/2001).

United States Department of Treasury. Historical Debt Outstanding Annual 2000-2007. http://treasurydirect.gov.NP/NPGateway (accessed 11/13/2008).

United States Energy Information Administration. Cushing, OK, Spot Price FOB. http://www.tonto.eia.doe.gov/dnav/pet/hist/rwtcd.htm (accessed 11/13/2008).

United States International Trade Commission. "Steel-Consuming Industries: Competitive Conditions With Respect To Steel Safeguard Measures" (Investigation No. 332-452). Volume III: Executive Summaries and Investigation No. 332-452 (Report and Appendices), Publication No. 3632. Washington, DC: USITC, 2003.

Veryser, Paul. "Manufacturing: Requirements for Recovery". Speech. University of Detroit Mercy. Sterling Heights, MI. November 1, 2008.

Viking Yachts History. http://www.vikingyachts.com/main/history.asp (accessed July 2, 2007).

Von Mises, Ludwig. *Socialism.* Indianapolis: LibertyClassics, 1979.

Wall Street Journal, "Good Riddance to the Luxury Tax," January 16, 2003.
——— "Mexico Retaliates," March 19, 2009.
——— " National Health Preview," March 27, 2009.

Wanniski, Jude. *The Way the World Works.* New York: BasicBooks, Inc. 1978.

Winik, Jay. *April 1865: The Month That Saved America.* New York: Perennial, 2002.

INDEX

ABOUT THE AUTHOR

David R. Breuhan is a Vice President and Portfolio Manager at the private investment firm of Gregory J. Schwartz & Co., Inc. in Bloomfield Hills, Michigan. He served as a commissioned officer in the United States Army attaining the rank of Captain. David served with the First Squadron, First Cavalry in West Germany and commanded B Troop, 1st Squadron, Third Armored Cavalry Regiment in Operation Desert Storm. He attended Airborne and Ranger training and The Canadian Land Warfare Command and Staff College.

David taught as an Adjunct Assistant Professor in the Department of Finance and Economics at Walsh College and is a guest lecturer at the University of Detroit Mercy. He has published in *Barron's*, *The Detroit News*, *Crain's Detroit Business*, *Marine Corps Gazette*, *Infantry Magazine* and *Defense Science*. David has been interviewed by Neil Cavuto, National Public Radio, Armed Forces Network and has appeared on the Mitch Albom Show. He has briefed the Vice President, Members of Congress and the United States International Trade Commission.

David received a Bachelor of Science degree from the United States Military Academy at West Point and a Master of Science in Finance from Walsh College.